ways

to manage
time effectively

Stella Cottrell

First published 2019 by
RED GLOBE PRESS

Red Globe Press in the UK is an imprint of Springer Nature Limited, registered in England, company number 785998, of 4 Crinan Street, London, N1 9XW.

Red Globe Press® is a registered trademark in the United States, the United Kingdom, Europe and other countries.

ISBN 978-1-352-00585-1 paperback

This book is printed on paper suitable for recycling and made from fully managed and sustained forest sources. Logging, pulping and manufacturing processes are expected to conform to the environmental regulations of the country of origin.

A catalogue record for this book is available from the British Library.

A catalog record for this book is available from the Library of Congress.

Contents

5O Ways

Acknowledgements

I would like to acknowledge my warmest thanks to those involved in the production of this book, especially Georgia Park and Amy Brownbridge for producing books within the series; Jayne Martin-Kaye for text design; Barbara Wilson for copyediting; Genevieve Friar for proofreading; and Helen Caunce for her oversight and support. I am especially grateful to Claire Dorer and Georgia Park for the innumerable tasks they have undertaken to enable the production of the series, their care over the details and their generous encouragement and goodwill.

"Clock" icon by Yurr, pp. 2, 10, 55; "Superhero" icon by Moriah Rich, p. 2; "Strength" icon by Cuby Design, p. 7; "Devil" icon by Deemak Daksina, p. 11; "Celebration" icon by Fantastic, p. 11; "Text message" by Artem Kovyazin, p. 11; "Game" icon by AFY Studio, p. 11; "Time management" icon by Aneeque Ahmed, p. 13; "Night" icon by Asianson.design, p. 13; "Solution" icon by Gregor Cresnar, p. 13; "Question" icon by Gregor Cresnar, p. 15; "Sunrise" icon by Mikicon, p. 16; "Key" icon by Mike Rowe, p. 17; "Listening" icon by MRFA, p. 19; "Scale" icon by Gregor Cresnar, p. 19; "Notes" icon by Vectors Market, p. 19; "Folder" icon by William, p. 21; "Alarm Clock" icon by Gregor Cresnar, p. 21; "Diary" icon by Creative Stall, p. 21; "Stopwatch" icon by Castor & Pollux, p. 23; "Footsteps" icon by Lukasz M. Pogoda, pp. 25, 99; "Signpost" icon by Gonzalo Bravo, p. 25; "Bus" icon by Clelia Colombo, p. 27; "Study" icon by Adrien Coquet, p. 27; "Thinking" icon by Hea Poh Lin, p. 27; "Jump" icon by Lluisa Iborra, p. 29; "Archery board" by Icon 54, p. 31; "Pine tree" by Rose Alice Design, p. 35; "Walk" icon by Adrien Coquet, p. 35; "Dream" icon by Adrien Coquet, p. 35; "Fast time" icon by Delwar Hossain, p. 37; "Timer" icon by Adnen Kadri, p. 41; "Pear" icon by Mario Bieh, p. 41; "Meditation" icon by Gan Khoon Lay, p. 41; "Notebook" icon by Andrejs Kirma, p. 45; "Lamp" icon by Ahmad Zeinuri, p. 45; "Reading" icon by Oleg Frolov, p. 45; "Laptop" icon by Miza Bin, p. 45; "Mug" icon by Arthur Shlain, p. 45; "Eye" icon by Octavio Cruz, p. 48; "Clock" icon by Mikicon, p. 51; "To do list" icon by Kamal, p. 53; "Do not disturb" icon by Scott Lewis, p. 55; "Study" icon by Adrien Coquet, p. 61; "Timer" icon by Dinosoft Labs, p. 65; "Deadline" icon by Ralf Schmitzer, p. 65; "Desk" icon by Nociconist, p. 67; "Team" icon by B Farias, p. 71; "Note" icon by Markus, p. 75; "Questions" icon by Gregor Cresnar, p. 75; "Arrow" icon by Adrien Coquet, p. 75; "Peoples Brainstorm" icon by Musmellow, p. 79; "Reminder" icon by Gregor Cresnar, p. 81; "Calendar" icon by Markus, p. 83; "Planning" icon by Gregor Cresnar, p. 83; "Phone" icon by Y. Onaldi, p. 83; "Books" icon by Mr Balind, p. 87; "Library" icon by Ayub Irawan, p. 87; "Kindle" icon by Prettycons, p. 87; "Notes" icon by Gregor Cresnar, p. 87; "List" icon by Alexander, p. 91; "Text message" icon by Rflor, p. 93; "Laptop" icon by I Cons, p. 93; "Post" icon by Adrien Coquet, p. 93; "Study" icon by Susannanova, p. 95; "Paper" icon by KD, p. 101; "Job" by Adrien Coquet, p. 103; "Document" icon by Dinosoft Labs, p. 103; "Timetable" icon by ProSymbols, p. 105; "Folders" icon by Creaticca Creative Agency, p. 105; "Sticky notes" icon by SBTS, p. 106; "Frustration" icon by Luis Prado, p. 106; "Backpack" icon by Dumitrui Robert, p. 105; "Rice" icon by Art Shop, p. 107; "Charger" icon by Alexander Skowalsky; all from the Noun Project (www.thenounproject.com).

About this book

This book suggests 50 Ways of making time work better for you as a student. It covers many aspects of time-management, including:

- Ways to think about and approach time-management in the context of student life

- Ways to use time more effectively

- Ways to use time to support your longer-term ambitions

- Ways to enjoy and benefit from your time as a student.

Just a taste …

This is a small book with many big ideas. Each 'Way' is a starting point, offering suggestions of things to do and to think about. Browse these to spark ideas of your own. You may find this small taste is enough in itself to spur you to action – or you can follow up suggestions using the resources recommended.

Map your own route

Studies show that good time management is individual to the person and situation: there isn't one method that suits everyone.[1,2]

As each student is different, the best combination of actions to take will be unique to you. Start with page ix, then select from the 50 Ways to suit your own needs and interests. Be open and adventurous in your approach: try out things you might not usually consider.

The 50 Ways series

This series is especially useful for students who want to dip into a book on an aspect of study or student life that is relevant to them at this point. The 50 Ways books are easy to carry around for a short burst of inspiration and motivation.

How to use this book

Get started
Begin with the introduction
and Ways 1–5.

Discover
Find out about different things that
people do to manage time.

Become more self-aware
Try out different things to learn about your own
patterns of time use and what works for you.

Reflect
Use the mini self-evaluations to focus your thinking. Then
consider possible ways forward suggested by your answers.

Choose
Decide which of the 50 Ways you want to try out. You don't
have to do them all!

Commit
Once you decide to commit to something, put your whole self
behind your decision. Do it!

Shape new habits
Make time-management a natural part of the way you study,
work and live. See page x.

Find out more
Follow up using the recommended resources if you wish. See pages
114–16 or use the reference list to follow up sources numbered in
superscript in the text.

Shape new habits and ways of thinking

Develop good habits for time management so that these become second nature, easing time pressures and enhancing your performance.

Act
Be active in shaping new habits and ways of thinking. Most pages of this book provide opportunities to reflect, choose, decide and commit.

Commit
Place yourself fully behind your good intentions by using the 'I will' boxes. Be selective: decide which are the most important actions for you now.

Track
Keep track of your good intentions. It takes time to form new habits so give it time. If you forget for a while, just come back to them. It gets easier each time. If you wish, you can use:

- pages 108–9 to track and monitor new habits you want to form

- pages 110–11 to track your progress with any of the Ways you try out

- pages 112–13 to keep note of your 20+ favourite time-saving tips, for easy access.

Don't wait until too late!
The earlier you start to manage your time, the more time you will have to enjoy the benefits (Way 2). If you keep putting it off, you reduce your options. It can also mean that you find yourself managing one crisis after another, rather than managing your time.

What is good time management?

Good time management means taking charge of how you organise your life, behaviour and thinking so that:

- you enjoy the time you have

- you are conscious of how you are using time

- you can feel happy in the future with the way you used time now

- you use time to best effect – depending on your circumstances

- you use time efficiently, avoiding time-wasting

- you reduce unnecessary time pressures and stresses

- you get things done – and on time

- you know, and achieve, your priorities

- you are in the right place at the right time

- you enable a good life/work balance – to the benefit of your study, career, work, health, relationships, well-being and happiness

- you get the rest, relaxation, sleep and downtime you need

- you can focus in the moment

- you plan for your future needs and interests

- you can cope independently

- you have time to think

- you have time to be yourself.

Why time management matters for students

Effective time management is an essential skill for students in higher education. Many studies associate it with better academic performance and higher grades as well as other benefits.[3,4,5,6]

At college and university, you are responsible for organising much of your own study time and for making sure you get everything done on time. That means taking charge of all kinds of study tasks and related administration. You need to fit in many commitments, such as jobs, social life, caring responsibilities, volunteering, sport, leisure activities, taking care of your health, well-being, security and everyday essentials.

All this requires substantial thought about how to juggle everything you need to do so that you carry these out in the best order, at the right time and for the right duration. It means shaping tasks to fit available time. You need to know when to save time and when not to cut corners.

It also means thinking ahead, planning and preparing for events that lie at different points in the future, such as assignment submission dates, exams, subject options, dissertation or research project topics, career choices, CV-building and graduate employment. You might need to work in groups for study projects or work placements where your time management affects other people and is affected by them.

Ineffective time management is at the root of many difficulties experienced by students. It can mean essential study tasks are not completed, or are completed poorly or under great stress.[7] It affects whether students complete the course on time and their grades.

The upside is that once you learn to manage time well, you gain much more control over your life, performance and achievement. This eases stress and provides you with valuable skills for life.

What does time management involve for students?

For students, good time management involves such things as:

- enjoying your overall experience as a student

- balancing study with a healthy lifestyle and other commitments

- gaining enjoyment from time spent studying

- optimising the learning gained during time spent in study

- pacing study well over time, in order to learn at your best without undue pressure, stress or anxiety

- making time for everything you need to do

- planning time out carefully and using your diary/planner well

- using the opportunities available during your time as a student

- attending all scheduled learning, arriving on time, staying until the end, and using class time as intended with focussed attention

- taking responsibility for organising unscheduled study time

- planning out assignments and study tasks carefully, starting these sufficiently early to deal with whatever might arise

- giving yourself sufficient time to think

- completing assignments and exams within the allocated time

- sorting out administrative and organisational tasks on time

- completing your course successfully and on time.

What is different about 'student time'?

Student time as a resource

Time is one of a student's most valuable resources – it is gold. You can't manufacture more minutes to the day, but you can create more time, in effect, through the way you use time, and by what you choose to do, or not to do, how and when.

Student time as a responsibility

Being in higher education entails a greater level of responsibility for managing study time than is typical at earlier stages. For many students, it is the first time that they have needed to consider the fine details of what to do now in order to keep everything on track for the short and longer term. It can mean that, suddenly, there is no one to do things that were done or organised for them previously, and no one to remind them of these either. They are not used to planning in detail from day to day, and across the week, month, term and year.

There are many assumptions about how students should use time, but it is up to each individual how to go about this. It is a personal decision whether to plan, organise, schedule, to be sorted or chaotic. Being in charge of time – all the time – can be experienced as an exciting freedom or, if not well-managed, as a source of anxiety.

Student time as a sensation

As there is a greater amount of unscheduled or independent study, it can seem as if time has little or no structure. It might feel as if time drifts or speeds up or slows down in curious ways. Students can feel as if their usual sense of a normal day, week, or month undergoes a change: last week seems as though it took place months ago and the end of the term seems further away than it is. The sense of urgency to take part in what is going on today can be much greater. The urgency to get things done for the future might fade.

Such changes in the sense of time can be disorientating and might even provoke anxiety. They can trick students into feeling as if time is 'endless' or that they have much more time to get things done than is the case. Good time management can help to anchor the sense of time more realistically.

Time as a pressure

There are times in the student year, and in some parts of the week, when it seems there are far too many things to fit into too little time. Without good time management, students can find that, suddenly, there are now several assignments to complete, exams to prepare for, events to attend, decisions to be made, and time to be found for socialising and everyday life as well. This can be experienced as exhilarating for some, and anxiety-provoking for others. Studies suggest that effective time management is associated with lower levels of anxiety.[7,8,9,10]

Time to account for …

Student time can feel like being in a bubble, unconnected to the future and the outside world to a large extent. However, once students apply for work as a graduate, potential employers are interested in how they used the time, resources and opportunities available to them. How they used these can make the difference in being considered for the jobs they want most. You might also find you want to account to your future self for what you did with all the valuable time you have had.

Time as a healthy rhythm

Our bodies run on a regular 24-hour clock of alert wakefulness and sleepiness, known as circadian rhythm or sleep/wake cycle. Typically, for adults, the greatest energy slumps occur at around 2–4 a.m. and 1–3 p.m., although it varies from person to person. You notice the effects of this more when you have underslept: you will find you are more tired at certain times of the day yet still relatively alert at others. Being aware of when your energy normally peaks and falls in the day can help you to plan study and other activities to suit your energy level.

The circadian rhythm is a strong internal mechanism. It is affected by light and dark and operates best on your behalf when you go to sleep and wake up at the same times every day, including weekends. Student life can disrupt the natural sleep/wake cycle, depriving you of good sleep and of prime times for being alert for efficient study. This can be because of the pressures of getting assignments in on time, revising for exams or joining in the intense social life. It is not unusual for students to 'pull all-nighters', working right through the night.

Whilst the occasional late night or lost night's sleep can be slept off later, it is unwise to disrupt your natural sleep pattern on a routine basis. You will feel better, and use time more effectively, if you become aware of your internal clock. Aim to establish a regular pattern of sleeping and working at your optimum times.[11]

Time is success

The way we spend our time, day by day and across many years, defines who we are and how we are perceived by others. It plays an important role in what we are able to achieve for ourselves.

Do justice to your studies

It can be hard to find the time you need to achieve everything of which you are capable as a student. How well you do isn't only a question of time management, but this does play a major role.

Your success is affected by many different aspects of time management, such as:

- your awareness of time and self-awareness of how you use time

- your attitudes towards time

- decisions you make about time, including the total hours you put into study and how you use the time you put aside for study

- how you spend your time when not studying – as this affects your health, mental alertness, concentration and stamina for study.

Do justice to your potential

Time management can sometimes feel like another chore. It takes up some of your valuable time. However, it does pay off. Students who manage time well achieve better grades and have more time for activities that contribute to their career and broader success.

Time management as an employability skill

Considerations about time and its use are important to most jobs, careers and businesses. Effective time planning can make or break a business. For nurses and medical staff, wasted time is time not spent with a patient or learning a new procedure, which affects patient care and could be a question of life and death.[12] For teachers, time wasted can affect pupils' attainment and life chances. For a company, missing a delivery deadline can mean loss of customers.

Awareness of the impact of time management

Your time management affects others. In the workplace, it can mean others are able to get on with their work and meet their time deadlines. Poor time use by one person can affect others' livelihoods.

Time courtesies count

Everyday courtesies matter – such as turning up, being on time and getting things done when you say you will. Apart from the financial costs of poor time use, such courtesies reflect the professionalism and brand of the business. Typically, employers ask tutors or former employers to provide details of absenteeism and punctuality when considering a candidate for a job. Your everyday time behaviours can influence your opportunities.

Efficient and effective use of time

As part of the appointment process, employers might set assessment tasks to see how much work you can do in a competent manner under timed conditions. It is useful to develop the ability to settle down quickly to tasks and to find and maintain your focus for tasks you undertake.

Employability skills and qualities gained through effective time management

The skills and qualities you can acquire through developing your time-management abilities whilst a student include many that are relevant to graduate jobs and careers. Consider these for your CV. Decide on good examples of where you demonstrate these, to discuss at interview.

Punctuality	Maintaining focus – so that time is well used
Self-management and self-reliance	Ability to organise and complete a task from start to finish
Ability to organise your own work	Perseverance – able to keep going over time
Diary-management and planning	Flexibility when circumstances change over time
Thinking ahead and forward planning	Organisational skills
Scheduling to fit in multiple commitments	Co-ordinating your time with other people's
Goal-setting and prioritising	Finding solutions to time-related problems
Being a 'self-starter' rather than waiting to be told what to do	Coping with time pressures

1

Take your time power

Gain a sense of control

How does this help?

It can feel that time is in charge – running away from us when we are busy, hanging heavy upon us when we are bored, elusive in its ways. That isn't the case: our own minds shape our experience of time, our own decisions affect what we achieve in the time we have. You can take charge of how you think about time, how you spend it, what you achieve in given amounts of time, even how time feels to you. Students who perceive that they have some power in relation to time tend to feel less agitated or dejected about study tasks and exams. They accomplish more of what they set out to do, feel more satisfied, and gain better grades.[13]

Considering your responses

If you feel that you are controlled or limited by the time available to you, take charge. You gain more from the time available if you take conscious steps to understand time, enjoy it, direct it, organise, plan, prioritise and monitor it well.

 See also Ways 6, 8, 14

 Do I …?

1. Do I feel time runs away from me?
   Yes ✓ **No** ☐

2. Do I feel limited by time?
   Yes ☐ **No** ✓

3. Do I reflect on my use of time?
   Yes ✓ **No** ☐

To do. I will …

Take charge of your experience of time

Select ✔ approaches below that could help you take charge of time.

☑ **Own your power**
Recognise you are in charge of how you use and experience it.

☑ **Make your own time decisions**
Don't be influenced by other people's poor time decisions.

☑ **Be time-aware**
Gain a better sense of how time is structured and flows. (See page xiv and Way 10.)

☑ **Think of time positively**
Find friendly ways of thinking about it. (See Ways 4 and 5.)

☑ **Make time meaningful and fun**
… if it is dull, it drags.

☑ **Don't wait to be told what to do**
Use your initiative to get things done and on time.

☑ **Be time-reflective**
Pause to consider your use of time and attitude towards it.

☑ **Use strategy and techniques**
Learn to organise and monitor time well.

☑ **Form good time habits**
Be systematic in changing your time-related behaviours.

? Do I ...?

1. Do I know how I would benefit from better time management longer-term?

   Yes ✓ **No**

2. Do I know how I could benefit from better time management now?

   Yes **No** ✓

3. Do I keep these potential benefits in mind, to spur me to action?

   Yes ✓ **No**

2

'What's in it for me?'

Enjoy the benefits

How does this help?

We are more likely to follow through on good intentions for time management or any other actions if we recognise benefits to ourselves – especially any immediate benefit. Time management skills have been positively associated with multiple benefits. These include better grades, greater study satisfaction, less stress and less sense of 'work overload'.[5,6,14,15] It is useful to strengthen your awareness of what you have to gain.

Considering your responses

If your responses suggest you are not clear about the potential benefits of improving your time management, then identify these for both the longer term and short term. Even if you do know the benefits, it is worth cementing your sense of the gains. Decide how you will keep these benefits in mind so that being conscious of them motivates you to action.

 See also Ways 6, 14, 32, 46

 To do. I will ...

Identify the potential gains for you

Decide ✔ which of these time-management benefits are relevant to you. Jot down others that matter to you. **Highlight** any of immediate benefit.

☑ Feeling more in control	☑ Enjoying my study more
☑ Less stress/pressure	☑ More time for career planning and CV-building
☑ Fewer crises/less rush	☑ A better quality of life
☑ Getting more done	☑ More time for social life, family, sports/leisure, etc.
☑ Getting things done on time	
☑ Making fewer errors	☑ Time to prepare for class
☐ Arriving for things on time	☐ Time to earn some money
☑ Achieving better grades	☑ Ability to cope in future jobs

Other things? Make a list!

3

Identify your time-management priorities

Identify time-management strengths and weaknesses

How does this help?

Most people are good at some aspects of time management, not so good at others. It is likely that you have some relevant strengths that have helped you get this far. Even if your time management feels chaotic to you, taking action in just a few priority areas can make a big difference. It is useful to reflect on where you manage time well, where you don't, and what kinds of changes would make the most difference to you, either immediately or longer term.

Considering your responses

If you don't already reflect on how you manage time, give some thought to which aspects of time management are relative strengths for you, and pinpoint where things start to go adrift. Such reflection is a useful habit to cultivate. As we enter new situations, time demands differ. If we are consciously aware of how well we use time, it becomes easier to identify priorities for altering our approach to fit the circumstances.

 See also Ways 1, 2, 4, 6

 Do I ...?

1. Do I reflect on the effectiveness of my time-management habits?

Yes ☐ No ☐

2. Do I have strengths in my current time-management habits?

Yes ☐ No ☐

3. Do I know what prevents me from managing my time well?

Yes ☐ No ☐

 To do. I will ...

Strengths and weaknesses in your current habits

Rate the following 25 statements on a scale of 0–4. Give a rating of 4 for statements that are highly typical of you, and 0 if not at all typical.

Item	Rating
1. I have good control over time	0 1 2 3 4
2. I know exactly where my time goes	0 1 2 3 4
3. I am happy about my use of time	0 1 2 3 4
4. I put sufficient time into my studies	0 1 2 3 4
5. I use good time-management strategies	0 1 2 3 4
6. I get things done without stressing about time	0 1 2 3 4
7. I plan, organise and schedule my time and study	0 1 2 3 4
8. I use my diary/planner well to manage time	0 1 2 3 4
9. I get as much study done as I intend to do	0 1 2 3 4

Item	Rating
10. I know how long each study task will take me	0 1 2 3 4
11. I pace study tasks well across the term/semester	0 1 2 3 4
12. I don't leave things to the last minute	0 1 2 3 4
13. I am good at getting going with study tasks	0 1 2 3 4
14. I am good at sticking with study tasks once started	0 1 2 3 4
15. I settle down to study quickly after breaks	0 1 2 3 4
16. I find ways of making study time enjoyable	0 1 2 3 4
17. I always arrive on time for class, appointments, etc.	0 1 2 3 4
18. I always prepare well for class	0 1 2 3 4
19. I stay focussed when studying and in class	0 1 2 3 4
20. I put time into checking work before submission	0 1 2 3 4
21. I always complete/submit my work on time	0 1 2 3 4
22. I pace exam time well	0 1 2 3 4
23. I balance well time for study, work, sleep and social life	0 1 2 3 4
24. I have quiet downtime for thought and reflection	0 1 2 3 4
25. I spend enough time on CV-building/employability	0 1 2 3 4
Total	

Reflection: Where does it all go 'horribly wrong'?

Whilst consideration of your time habits is still fresh in your mind, reflect on where things start to go wrong. Jot down your thoughts here or on the Notes pages.

Interpret your results

75–100 If your ratings are accurate, then your time management looks excellent already. Use the 50 Ways to fine-tune your skills further.

50–74 Your ratings suggest you have good time-management ability. Use your ratings to identify priorities to increase your effectiveness.

0–49 Your ratings suggest there is a lot you could do to make time work better for you. It is worth rethinking your approach to time.

Act on your ratings and reflection

Your low-ratings are your 'hot spots' – areas for taking action.

1. **Follow up.** Whatever your rating, don't just put it aside.

2. **Consider.** Which changes could make you feel happier and more effective in your use of time?

3. **Reflect.** Why don't you do these things already? How can you take that into consideration in deciding on your action?

4. **Prioritise.** Identify 2–3 initial actions that would make a difference.

5. **Record.** Use page 108. Use a planner/diary to identify times for actions, for reminding yourself of your intentions and for checking on your progress.

6. **Do it.** Follow through on your decisions.

4

Know your time demons

Catch them in the act!

How does this help?

Our 'time demons' are the thinking patterns that divert us from our best intentions for time management. These patterns can serve us well in some situations. It is good to have in our lives some element of what they represent for us, such as rest, fun, curiosity and pursuit of excellence. They become troublesome only if they intrude excessively or at the wrong times. We may be prey to one time demon or many. If we are aware of the thinking patterns that undermine our time effectiveness, we can make conscious choices to change those patterns or act to mitigate their effect.

Considering your responses

If you are not sure about your time demons, consider the examples opposite. Become more aware of when and why such thought patterns arise for you. When are they helpful – and when not? What thought patterns would be more useful for you? Jot these down and use them.

 See also Ways 1, 3, 13, 45

? Do I ...?

1. Do I know what kinds of thought patterns undermine my time management?

   Yes ☐ No ☐

2. Do I notice quickly when I divert from good time management?

   Yes ☐ No ☐

3. Do I know my time-wasting behaviours?

   Yes ☐ No ☐

To do. I will ...

Which are your time demons?

Identify ✔ your own time demons.

☐ **'Later!' demon**
Takes away a sense of urgency. Encourages procrastination.

☐ **'Fun' demon**
Wants fun. Gets bored quickly, especially when sitting still.

☐ **'Distractor' demon**
Prevents you from concentrating, especially in class or if studying.

☐ **'Excessive breaks' demon**
Wants too many breaks or makes timely breaks last too long.

☐ **'What's new?' demon**
Curious about what is going on elsewhere. Wants to keep checking messages and media.

☐ **'Fascinator' demon**
Keeps you fascinated in what you are doing so you don't stop and move onto other activities when you should. This demon especially loves games and social media.

☐ **'Perfectionist' demon**
Makes you go over and over an aspect of a task, sucking up all available time and not letting you move on to other things.

Other time demons? Note them here!

5

Make friends with time

Time is not the enemy

How does this help?

People often act as if 'time' were an enemy with which they have to battle continually. There isn't enough time. Time is a problem. Time puts them under pressure. This way of thinking can be exhausting. There are more helpful ways to relate to time. It is because of time that we get to do all the things we enjoy, to be with people who matter to us, to learn new things, to make a difference in the world. If we have too much to do, we can look for solutions elsewhere rather than blaming time. Instead of seeing time as a problem, regard it as positive, precious, a friend to value.

Considering your responses

If your responses suggest that you take time for granted when your diary seems emptier but battle it when you have a lot to do, then make time your new best friend. Improve your planning so that study tasks, revision and other commitments are spaced more evenly over a longer period.

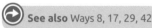 **See also** Ways 8, 17, 29, 42

 Do I ...?

1. Do I complain a lot about 'time'?

   Yes ☐ No ☐

2. Do I blame 'time' when I can't get something done?

   Yes ☐ No ☐

3. Do I take 'time' for granted when I am less busy?

   Yes ☐ No ☐

 Find out more

Mindfulness for Students, Cottrell (2018)[16]

 To do. I will ...

Keep time on your side

Value time as precious
Don't wish it away. Tune into the immediate moment and make it count in some way.

Get in rhythm with time
Be aware of when in the day you are at your best for getting different things done. Be mindful of natural rhythms that support our health, well-being and effectiveness. See page xvi.

Be grateful for busy times
Consider what it would mean if you didn't have study, work and those other commitments. You wouldn't still have the opportunities these bring either. What would you miss out on?

Reduce pressure on time
If 'time' is under pressure, be kind to it. Look for ways of easing the strain on it. Set clearer priorities. Look for time-saving solutions. Ask for help in sharing the workload. Delegate. Pace tasks better.

Be in the moment
Appreciate fully the time you have. Focus attention fully on tasks as you do them, noticing them more. It can bring greater calm and pleasure to them.[16]

6 Spend time where you will value it the most

Decide what you want from your time – direct it where it matters

How does this help?

It is worth looking at where you actually spend your time and consider whether that aligns with what you value – your future, your health, your friends, your grades, etc. Check whether the time you spend on different study tasks is really paying off. Could you spend that time better? According to the Pareto Principle, around 80% of what we achieve is undertaken in about 20% of our time. In other words, we spend the bulk of our time on things that end up having little real value to the outcome. That is fine if you value the time spent for other reasons. Be conscious of what you are gaining from the way you use time.

Considering your responses

If your responses suggest you don't spend time where it is most valuable to you, or don't really think about time in this way, then you could gain from doing so. Decide your priorities and the amount of time you want to devote to these – to avoid regrets later.

 See also Ways 2, 9, 14, 32

 Do I ...?

1. Do I think the 80/20 principle applies to the way I spend study time?

   Yes ☐ No ☐

2. Do I reflect on the value of time spent on each aspect of assignments?

   Yes ☐ No ☐

3. Do I often wish I had spent time differently?

   Yes ☐ No ☐

 Find out more

The Study Skills Handbook, Cottrell (2019)[17]

 To do. I will …

Question your use of time

Ask yourself what you value

- How much of your time should you give to these things?

- How much time do you spend on them at the moment?

List your priorities

- How much of your time do you think you should spend on each of these?

- How much do you usually spend on them?

Is this the best use of my time?

- Ask yourself this before making time commitments.

- Ask yourself this during tasks – decide whether to change task.

- Ask after the event – are you happy you made the best use of your time?

Check your use of time

- Reflect on how you spent your time today – or this week, this year, in this class, on this project.

- What does your time use suggest about what you really value doing?

Do I ...?

1. Do I make rushed decisions?

   Yes ☐ **No** ☐

2. Do I use the best time of day for the right kind of decision?

   Yes ☐ **No** ☐

3. Do I lose out because I decide too late?

   Yes ☐ **No** ☐

7 Make well-timed decisions

Right decisions made at the right time

How does this help?

The timing of decisions affects the options open to us, as well as our levels of enjoyment, honesty, accuracy and speed. Too late, and you miss opportunities. Too early, and you might lack essential information. The time of day is also relevant to decision-making. Research suggests we make slower but more accurate decisions in the morning, and faster, less accurate ones later in the day.[18] We are more likely to make honest, ethical decisions in the morning when energised and rested.[19] Decisions that require self-control are also best when energised, such as after breaks and meals.[20] We can time tasks at the best times for the kinds of decisions involved.

Considering your responses

If you find decision-making difficult, consider the best time and timing for the sorts of decisions you need to make. Once you are well informed about your options, consider whether you need to delay any further.

 **See also** Ways 10, 11, 13, 17

 To do. I will ...

Timing is the key

Select ✔ which approaches to decision-making would be most helpful for you.

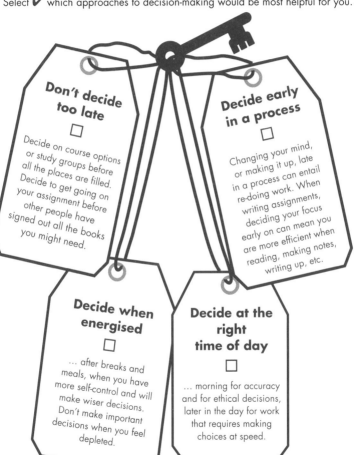

Don't decide too late

☐

Decide on course options or study groups before all the places are filled. Decide to get going on your assignment before other people have signed out all the books you might need.

Decide early in a process

☐

Changing your mind, or making it up, late in a process can entail re-doing work. When writing assignments, deciding your focus early on can mean you are more efficient when reading, making notes, writing up, etc.

Decide when energised

☐

... after breaks and meals, when you have more self-control and will make wiser decisions. Don't make important decisions when you feel depleted.

Decide at the right time of day

☐

... morning for accuracy and for ethical decisions, later in the day for work that requires making choices at speed.

8

Tune in to your time wisdom

Be time-reflective

How does this help?

As well as using strategies, methods and time-saving techniques, we can pay more attention to our own time wisdom. If we pause and reflect upon the way we use time, most of us are wise to our own time-management flaws and can think quite easily of things we could do to use time more effectively. We may not want to listen to our own time wisdom, as it is likely to tell us to get on with things we know we should be doing – or to wait before doing things we want to do right now. Ultimately, when you do use time effectively, it is your own time wisdom that has triumphed.

Considering your responses

If you already give yourself good advice and follow it, then you have an advantage. Way 3 is useful for checking areas where you tune in better, or worse, to your time wisdom. If you ignore your inner time warnings about study, work or CV-building, consider whether it is worth losing the benefits that your time wisdom is alerting you to.

 See also Ways 3, 4, 6, 22, 33

 Do I ...?

1. Do I give myself or others advice on how to manage time better?

   Yes ☐ **No** ☐

2. Do I ignore my own best advice?

   Yes ☐ **No** ☐

3. Do I know why I don't tune in to my time wisdom when I could?

   Yes ☐ **No** ☐

 To do. I will ...

Listen to your own best advice

Make space to listen

When you know there are things that must be done, make a point of creating quiet space to let your wise voice be heard. Don't keep drowning it out with noise, activity, worry and 'stuff'.

Notice the messages

When you recall there are things that need to be done, tune in to that alert. Ask yourself what exactly has to be done and by when. If you don't recall, then check the details straightaway.

Engage muscle memory

Jot it down. If you have already written an action into your diary, jot down the aspects you are going to undertake today, or straightaway.

Balance the benefits

Recognise that there are always benefits to doing and to not doing something – even if you don't immediately register what these are. Work out the benefits you gain either way, and weigh up what really matters to you.

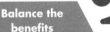

9

Use the right 'time tools'

Get equipped to manage time

 Do I ...?

1. Do I get up as soon as my alarm goes off in the morning?

   Yes ☐ No ☐

2. Do I investigate new study apps to see if they can save me time?

   Yes ☐ No ☐

3. Do I use my diary/planner well to keep my life organised?

   Yes ☐ No ☐

How does this help?

A few basic tools can make a big difference to how well you organise your time. Just an alarm clock, a good diary/planner and an up-to-date 'to-do' list take you a long way if used well. Experiment with study and time-saving apps to see what works for your style of doing things. Select a handful that really save time; avoid wasting time on app hunting. The value of your 'time tools' is more about using them well rather than having many of them. Look out for round-ups of latest study apps each year.[21]

Considering your responses

This is relatively easy to sort. Clocks, alarms and planners are cheap and easily available and there are many free study apps. Look for items you can set up quickly and that suit your style of working, so they save you time rather than becoming diversions from study.

 Find out more

The Macmillan Student Planner (Cottrell)[21] includes an annual update of time-saving apps.

 To do. I will ...

 See also Ways 26, 44, 50

Put your time tools to good use!

Use an alarm clock

Supplement the alarms on your phone. Put the alarm in a place that makes you get up (or at least move) to switch it off.

Use an academic diary

… to plan and organise study time.

- Keep it up to date.
- Check throughout the day.
- Attach your daily 'to-do' list.

Plan assignments into your diary

Break assignments down into study tasks, such as reading, researching, writing drafts, etc. Write each step into your diary.

Plan CV-building into your diary

Make specific time available for activities that relate to career planning, professional development and CV-building.

Quick information storage

Although writing notes by hand is good for learning and recall, apps such as Evernote can be great 'scrapbooks'. Use for collecting into one place thoughts, images, documents, websites, PDFs, etc. in a visual, multi-format way.

Use quick referencing apps

… such as Zotero and Mendeley (see page 114).

Use stationery as a time-tool

Use folders, dividers, highlighters and labels to find information at speed.

Do I ...?

1. Do I understand the time demands there will be later in the year?

   Yes ☐ **No** ☐

2. Do I find time 'drags' sometimes?

   Yes ☐ **No** ☐

3. Do I plan my work to avoid time pressures later in the year?

   Yes ☐ **No** ☐

10

Learn the flow of the academic year

Gain a sense of the ebb and flow of time across the year

To do. I will ...

How does this help?

Students often find that time seems to flow differently in higher education. The scheduling of classes, the amount of autonomous study and the pacing of assignments can make it seem as if time crawls early in the year. This can trick you into thinking you have plenty of time – then deadlines arrive faster than expected. Typically, times with little scheduled teaching are for preparing assignments and learning material for exams. Understanding the way time operates on your course helps you to pace your work across the year, avoiding serious time problems later. Use apparently 'slow' or unscheduled time earlier in the year for background study, revision and preparation.

Considering your responses

If you are not already taking steps to ease time pressures later in the year, start now. If time moves slowly, make use of unscheduled time to prepare for assignments, exams, CV-building and career development.

 See also Ways 11, 12, 30, 42

Feel it in the bones!

Decide ✔ which ideas would be useful for you to follow up.

Make a 'full field' list
… of everything you want and need to do in this study year, across all aspects of your life. Gain a sense of just how much there is to do.

Use a wall planner
… to map out tasks for achieving your list: see the year at a glance.

Know start and finish dates
- for the academic year
- for vacations and study weeks
- for placements (if applicable)
- for tests and exams

Know other key dates
- for welcome/induction
- for submitting assignments
- for reading weeks
- for course events

Ask previous students
In retrospect, which parts of the year seemed to race by?

Think it through
Reflect on the implications of how you spend time early in the year, in 'slower times' and in vacation weeks. Gain a good sense of the whole year.

11

Take time to adapt to the course

Give yourself time to settle

How does this help?

The transition into higher education or a new year of study can be harder than expected. It can take time to find out how everything works, to make friends, feel you belong and to gain a sense of what tutors want. If you had great friends and good grades in the past, it can be unsettling if everything doesn't fall into place straightaway. Some students lose valuable time worrying about what seems wrong rather than taking things in stages and giving themselves time to adapt. Over time, the probability is that your course, its culture and expectations will become familiar, you'll bond with others and feel 'at home'.

Considering your responses

If your responses suggest that you are being hard on yourself and worrying about getting everything right straightaway, then be kinder to yourself. Set personal goals for settling in – and allow yourself time.

 Do I ...?

1. Do I feel anxious about how long it is taking me to settle into my course?

   Yes ☐ **No** ☐

2. Do I worry that I don't feel at home on my course?

   Yes ☐ **No** ☐

3. Do I feel I won't last the course?

   Yes ☐ **No** ☐

 Find out more

The Study Skills Handbook, Cottrell (2019)[17]

 To do. I will ...

 See also Ways 7, 10, 12, 19

Achieve study and personal milestones

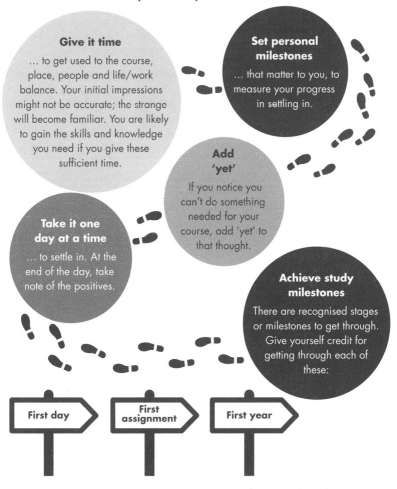

Give it time
… to get used to the course, place, people and life/work balance. Your initial impressions might not be accurate; the strange will become familiar. You are likely to gain the skills and knowledge you need if you give these sufficient time.

Set personal milestones
… that matter to you, to measure your progress in settling in.

Add 'yet'
If you notice you can't do something needed for your course, add 'yet' to that thought.

Take it one day at a time
… to settle in. At the end of the day, take note of the positives.

Achieve study milestones
There are recognised stages or milestones to get through. Give yourself credit for getting through each of these:

First day

First assignment

First year

12 Create a realistic study timetable

Take a professional approach to your study timetable

How does this help?

Your study timetable is the basis for all your other life-planning if you are a full-time student. If you study part time and have to prioritise your job, it is still important to plan how student life and professional development will fit into your schedule. A good study timetable helps time-planning as most class times are fixed, at least during term-time. These provide an anchor for timing all your other activities. It is wise to schedule regular slots for important activities that could otherwise get squeezed out, including times for independent study and career planning.

Considering your responses

If you don't know when you are going to fit in important aspects of life, study or career development, allocate specific slots for these in your week. This will show you what is realistic. Make good decisions about where to allocate time on your timetable – then honour these.

 See also Ways 7, 16, 17, 44

 Do I ...?

1. Do I know what I am supposed to be doing at any given time?

   Yes ☐ No ☐

2. Do I schedule independent study?

   Yes ☐ No ☐

3. Do I have a good study/life balance?

   Yes ☐ No ☐

4. Do I know when I am going to fit in career-planning and CV-building?

   Yes ☐ No ☐

 To do. I will ...

Make a timetable that works for you

Write in regular slots

... for class times, employment, student societies, clubs, sports, family commitments, independent study, revision, CV-building, breaks and downtime. Don't forget travel time!

With study/life balance

Build in time for life essentials such as eating, sleeping and socialising.

With enough thinking time

You can always benefit from more thinking time!

Synchronise

Synchronise your study timetable with your diary, wall-planner (if you use one), and reminder-setting.

Stick to it

Follow through on your timetable, even if you don't feel like it. Treat it as if it were part of a job – act like a professional.

Necessary flex?

Leave some contingency time for emergencies. Timetable enough time to make up any study you miss.

13 Manage your procrastination

Take pressure off the scary tasks!

 Do I ...?

1. Do I put myself under pressure by putting things off continually?

   Yes ☐ **No** ☐

2. Do I tend to think it will be easier to get things done later?

   Yes ☐ **No** ☐

3. Do I find it hard to make myself do things even when I know I should?

   Yes ☐ **No** ☐

How does this help?

Procrastination means continually deferring tasks to the future, often with the rationalisation that your future self will be in a better position to do them. Procrastinators tend to prefer others to think they just didn't try rather than that they lack ability.[22] Studies suggest procrastination is mainly about mood regulation, especially when there seems to be more emotional enjoyment, or less task aversion, in doing nothing.[23,24] Everyone puts things off at times, but serious procrastination leads to stress, illness and poor grades.[25]

Considering your responses

If you are a procrastinator, it can be difficult to break the habit. It may help to get professional support for the first steps. The good news is that the best way forward involves finding more fun in study, and taking the choice out of whether you can do something or not.

 To do. I will ...

 See also Ways 8, 18, 21, 39, 45

Entice yourself to do it

Make tasks fun
Turn them into a game or find ways of building a 'feel good' factor into doing them – to gain some instant gratification from the task itself.

Make tasks smaller
Break tasks into tiny steps you can complete easily. It is easier to do more once you can see progress.

Reward your early bird
Reward yourself for getting things done ahead of your schedule.

Forgive your mess-ups
Feeling guilty about procrastination makes it worse.
Forgiving yourself helps you do better next time.[26]

Use a strong routine
… to help start tasks 'on autopilot'. Don't leave yourself any option except to do it.

Identify with 'future you'
A strong visual image of your future self can help you identify with the 'future you' that will benefit from what you do now.[27]

'I don't feel like it, but I am going to get started now!'
Acknowledge this if you still don't want to do it. Start with just a bit …

14

Be guided by your goals

Use goals to give direction to time planning

 Do I ...?

1. Do I set clear goals for study?

   Yes ☐ **No** ☐

2. Do I refer to my goals when planning my time?

   Yes ☐ **No** ☐

3. Do I use my goals to help me evaluate how well I am using my time?

   Yes ☐ **No** ☐

How does this help?

Goal-setting is a standard time management technique. You can set ambitious goals that stretch you to achieve more or, if you prefer, set goals you know you can meet or exceed. Choose the approach that motivates you best. As well as using goals to direct you for the long term, set smaller goals, 'milestones' or targets to achieve in the short term. These can be for the term, month, week, day or independent study session. Once set, your goals provide direction for your use of time, priorities and decision-making. Use your goals to guide and evaluate your use of time.

 Find out more

The Study Skills Handbook, Cottrell (2019)[17]

Considering your responses

If you are clear about your study goals, it can be easier to stay motivated throughout the course. It is easier to focus during study sessions if your purpose is clear. If you have set goals already, use them to direct your time management so that you align your actions with your intentions.

 To do. I will ...

 See also Ways 7, 13, 17, 20

Clarify purpose

Decide ✔ which of the actions you will follow up.

Set time-bound goals...
- to achieve whilst a student
- for assignments
- for CV-building
- for life

Be ambitious but realistic.

List what you need to do
List everything needed to achieve your goals.

Calculate time needed
… to complete each item on the list.

Plan the best order
Reorganise your list so tasks are in the most logical order. Think about things that you may need to put into motion early on, so that you are able to start and complete other tasks when you get to them.

Set many small goals
… to achieve the tasks that support your larger goals. Accomplishing these helps you to recognise your progress.

Schedule specific time actions
… to achieve goals. Write these into your diary/planner.

Monitor your time use
… to keep on schedule.

15

Style your day

Set the flavour of how you will experience time across the day

How does this help?

However pressurised our time, we can make conscious choices about the tone we want to set for the day. This shapes our day as chaotic or organised, rushed or well-paced, agitated or calm, happy or miserable, pressurised or taken in our stride. Decide on 2–3 things you will definitely get done – then prepare your day in advance so you achieve these. You can take steps to give your day a distinctive style – as positive, organised and well-paced. The way you start the day and the attitude you bring to it shapes your experience of time, so ensure it is the experience you want!

Considering your responses

If your answers suggest that you leave the flavour of your day to chance, then do more to set its tone and shape its character. Your experience of time starts in the mind and is shaped by your actions.

 See also Ways 6, 14, 17, 22

 Do I ...?

1. Do I plan my day so that it flows well?

   Yes ☐ **No** ☐

2. Do I make conscious decisions about the kind of day I am going to have?

   Yes ☐ **No** ☐

3. Do I prepare in advance to help ensure that my day works out much as I want?

   Yes ☐ **No** ☐

 Find out more

Mindfulness for Students, Cottrell (2018)[16]

 To do. I will ...

Shape your experience of the day

Decide ✔ which actions to take.

Set priorities for the day in advance
What are you determined to achieve tomorrow?

Give yourself a boost
Plan out your day so that you will be able to recognise achievements or progress by its end.

Prepare the night before
- Check and prepare your planner
- Prepare your bag, ready to go!
- Lay out your clothes
- Set the alarm with just enough time to get everything done.

Start the day well
Get up and get going promptly when the alarm goes. Don't rush. Eat well. Check your planner. Take a moment of calm to settle your mind.

Decide the day's tone
Whatever you feel when you wake up, decide the attitude and ways of responding you will adopt for the rest of the day – to be effective and content. Set yourself reminders.

Leave breathing space
… in your day, so you are not completing everything in a rush. Build in time to work around things that don't go to plan – and for some 'downtime'.

Shape the flow
… of activity and rest across the day depending on when you do the most intense work, and the lengths and types of breaks you need.

16

Plan enough downtime

Make time to stop, to dream, to breathe ...

 Do I ...?

1. Do I tend to fill my days with activity?

   Yes ☐ **No** ☐

2. Do I have a regular, uninterrupted, sleep pattern?

   Yes ☐ **No** ☐

3. Do I give my brain time to refresh?

   Yes ☐ **No** ☐

How does this help?

'Downtime' for rest, calm, daydreaming and sleep is essential for good functioning of the brain as well as for health and mental health. It supports learning, memory, metabolism, stamina and physical energy. Our circadian rhythms are set so that we function best if our sleep occurs at night.[28] A regular sleep cycle boosts academic performance.[29] The occasional night of disrupted sleep (such as for a party or to complete an assignment) won't do much harm, but isn't the best strategy. When we sleep, rest and daydream, our brains remain active in searching out answers, making sense of new material and laying down memories.[30]

Considering your responses

If you tend to pack your days with similar tasks that require focussed thought, then use your diary to book time for good sleep, catching up on sleep you know you'll miss, and for varied kinds of downtime. A more balanced use of time will help body and brain to work more effectively.

 To do. I will ...

 See also Ways 12, 15, 36

It's not all go! go! go!

Sleep at least 7–8 hours
Students who achieve well have been found to sleep more – averaging around 9 hours a night.

Sleep to help recall
Your brain recalls material better after sleeping on it.

Schedule 'downtime'
… during the day and week, to free your brain up to do its job.

Find 'breathing time'
A break, a walk, sports, daydreaming or domestic tasks – anything that doesn't involve focussed thought can be 'buffer time' between tasks. That refreshes the brain and lets it work out things on its own.

Send your brain on errands
Tell it what to work on for you during downtime, whilst you are not paying attention to that task.

Appreciate downtime
It is a wonderful thing. You get to rest or have fun, whilst continuing to learn.

17

Use smart pacing and forward planning

Start early to benefit from long lead-in times

How does this help?

On most courses, it is assumed that you will pace your learning evenly across the course or year. There is usually a long lead-in to assignments to give you plenty of time to research, plan, write and think. Whilst you can rush some tasks, this is a poor strategy and won't work for complex or larger assignments. Revision for exams, career-planning or deciding on a topic for your dissertation/special paper are all best started early and paced over a longer period. This helps you to fit in everything you need to do and to benefit from opportunities that arise early in the year.

Considering your responses

If you complete major tasks in one go rather than paced over time, you deprive yourself of essential time to think, reflect, comprehend, absorb, generate ideas, review, correct, and fine-tune so that your work does you justice. If you start early on revision, CV-building and on large tasks, you pick up earlier on potential problems and opportunities.

 See also Ways 12, 42, 47, 48

 Do I ...?

1. Do I use 'all-nighters' for assignments?

   Yes ☐ **No** ☐

2. Do I leave time between drafts of my work so I return to it with fresh eyes?

   Yes ☐ **No** ☐

3. Do I spread tasks such as revision and career-planning across the year?

   Yes ☐ **No** ☐

 Find out more

The Study Skills Handbook, Cottrell (2019)[17]

 To do. I will ...

No last minute-ism!

Decide ✔ which actions would benefit your study.

Take an early look
... at what is coming up later in the year.
Check what you can begin early to ease pressure later.

Sound out the terrain
Get a feel for what is really involved. Browse topics so you know which involve most reading, thought or time off-campus.

Ask previous students
In retrospect, what do they wish they had started earlier?

Start assignments early
Give yourself time to make sense of what is involved and fine-tune your work, without needing to rush.

Plan 'backwards'
Work backwards from deadlines and exam dates to fit in all the time you need for study, thought and for fine-tuning assignments.
Use this to work out when to begin.[17]

Visit the careers service
Do this early in the year so that you are alert to the best opportunities for CV-building and jobs, and the best times to get things done.

Start exam prep early
You can't start too early in mastering the course material.[31]
See Ways 42 and 48.

18

Speed-task it!

Set yourself time challenges

(?) Do I ...?

1. Do I spend too long getting going on tasks then have to rush to finish?

   Yes ☐ No ☐

2. Do I assume important tasks have to take a long time to get right?

   Yes ☐ No ☐

3. Do I feel adrift wondering where to begin on new assignments/projects?

   Yes ☐ No ☐

How does this help?

Whilst it is important to plan sufficient time to complete tasks well, that doesn't mean we must then use it all. Often, if we take a small slice of the time available and set ourselves a task to complete at super-speed, our brains find a way to do it. This first attempt might be good enough. Typically, it provides a useful foundation to build upon. Used that way, speed-tasking can save time and reduce the pressure of getting started. Speed-tasking is a great way to begin a plan, a study session, a new stage in a larger task or writing a first draft of a paragraph or assignment.

Considering your responses

If you tend to labour over tasks, especially at the start or when planning, then set yourself a challenging time limit to complete a first attempt. Be prepared for some weak or odd aspects to such a rushed plan. Identify the gems in what you produce and work on those in more detail.

To do. I will ...

➔ See also Ways 20, 21, 23, 39, 45

Beat the clock!

Set a challenging limit
… such as 60 seconds or 2–3 minutes for a task to which you usually allocate much longer.

Have a go at a …
- 60-second 'to-do' list
- 60-second study session plan
- 3-minute attempt at generating ideas for a project
- 2-minute essay plan
- 3-minute information search
- 3-minute Conclusion
- 3-minute Introduction
- 5-minute draft essay

Make a smart start
Set a timer and get going. See how much you can get done in the time.

Select
Read your rapid response. Delete anything you don't want to keep. Look for ideas and phrases you could use or work on further.

Repeat
Repeat the challenge. See whether different ideas or phrases emerge.

Provide incubation time
Focus on something else for a while. Give your brain time to incubate the ideas it was working on for the speed task.

Fresh eyes
Look again at what you produced. After a break, the potential flaws will stand out more, giving you something to work on to take the task forward.

19

Build study stamina

Extend your attention span for study

How does this help?

There are many studies and theories about the optimum time to stay on task; typically, these suggest 20–50 minutes. In practice, it is highly individual to the person and task. Seasoned students can study effectively for many hours at a time with fewer and shorter breaks. They move flexibly between different kinds of study tasks within a single sitting – planning, reading, thinking, writing, checking, note-making – which breaks up the time. Time away from task can be great for re-energising yourself. Some people find breaks disrupt their train of thought and waste time. It takes time to become re-absorbed in what you were doing. You can build your study stamina so that you learn to work effectively for longer.

Considering your responses

Take the kind of breaks you need to reboot your energy for study, and without feeling guilty. Develop your awareness of the kind of breaks you need for sustained effective study. See if you can build your stamina gradually towards longer periods of study, with or without breaks.

 See also Ways 16, 27, 34, 39

 Do I ...?

1. Do I feel guilty if I take breaks?

   Yes ☐ No ☐

2. Do I take too many breaks?

   Yes ☐ No ☐

3. Do I find it takes me time to settle back to study after a break?

   Yes ☐ No ☐

4. Do I feel energised by breaks?

   Yes ☐ No ☐

 Find out more

Mindfulness for Students, Cottrell (2018)[16]

 To do. I will ...

Build your study muscle!

Build gradually

Aim to build study stamina slowly over your course. Add an extra minute or two, then a few more.

Set a timer

Focus only on study until the timer sounds. Gradually increase the time you set.

Find the optimum duration

… for you to study effectively. It could vary depending on what you are doing and the time of day.

Change is as good as a rest

Alternate between different study tasks on the same theme rather than always taking a break.

Vary your breaks

Plan for quick breaks between short tasks, as well as longer breaks for food, exercise, class, rest and socialising.

Tune in to your needs

If your attention starts to wander or your energy drops, give your brain a rest from that task or decide the kind of break you need.

Follow your energy

If you are focussed on what you are doing, keep going even if you had planned a break.

Mindfulness first

Spending a few minutes in meditation or taking a nap can build stamina for extended study.[16]

20

Break it down!

How does this help?

The thought of preparing for an important exam, writing a presentation or completing an assignment can feel overwhelming. For these and other large tasks, it is easier to break the task down into component parts. Treat each of these as a task in its own right, and assign times for starting and completing it into your diary. Map your progress towards the endpoint of the task as a whole, checking off tasks as you complete them. Pause to take account of how completed tasks contribute to the whole. Take note of how you are moving forwards towards completion with each step.

Considering your responses

If you waste time getting started because you feel overwhelmed by the task, it can help to divert your focus from the endpoint for a while and concentrate on the first steps. Once you get going, the overall task will seem more manageable. Every journey starts with a single step!

 Do I ...?

1. Do I tend to delay starting tasks because I don't know where to begin?

   Yes ☐ No ☐

2. Do I feel overwhelmed by the length of assignments?

   Yes ☐ No ☐

3. Do I worry about my capacity to complete large and complex tasks?

   Yes ☐ No ☐

 Find out more

Dissertations and Project Reports, Cottrell, (2014)[32]

 To do. I will ...

 See also Ways 13, 22, 24, 34

Divide large tasks into bite-sized ones

List the steps

Make a list of all the main steps in the process. Time spent working these out helps you to become familiar with the task, reducing fear of the unknown.

Know the steps

If you are unsure of the task, such as for a first essay or a larger project or dissertation, use a specialist guide that helps you to identify these. See pages 114–15.

Map out the whole

Make a big chart or map of all the things that have to be done. Use arrows to link tasks that connect or follow on from others. Make the map colourful and visual. Reflect on the whole so that you become familiar with how it all fits together.

Number tasks

... in the best order for completing them. Sort these into a list. Make a time in your diary for each item on the list. Having a given number of things to do, even if large, allows your brain to register that there is a finite list – there is an end to it!

Decide on quick wins

Look for a few easy things you can do straightaway. Do them. Gain confidence from knowing you have got the task or project underway.

Take stock of your progress

... on a regular basis. Recognise the things you have finished from your list. Celebrate the milestones!

21

Cue yourself in!

How does this help?

Your mind gets used to the actions associated with a routine. After a while, it recognises these as a sequenced pattern and performs them on 'autopilot'. Many students find it hard to settle at the beginning of a study session, wasting valuable time. If you find it takes you time to settle, focus and concentrate, create a strong routine to use every time you study. It could consist of one or several short tasks such as those listed on page 46. Through repetition, your brain will come to recognise these as your cue to start studying and cease distracting thoughts.

Considering your responses

If your responses suggest that you might benefit from establishing a strong pattern of actions as your cue to starting study, then this is an easy action to start today. Your routine will become your mind's cue for getting down to business quickly, so you can use your available time more effectively.

 Do I ...?

1. Do I find it hard to settle to study?

   Yes ☐ No ☐

2. Do I waste time when starting study?

   Yes ☐ No ☐

3. Do I have an established routine to cue me into study?

   Yes ☐ No ☐

 To do. I will ...

 See also Ways 18, 22, 34, 39

Build a strong study routine

Countdown: 3, 2, 1, go!

Realistic and workable?

Choose a set of actions you could easily perform for each study session. See page 46 for cues used by other students. Add your own.

List them – until they are automatic

Jot down your actions – either in words or as a visual list. Put this where you will see it. If necessary, place copies strategically where you can't miss them.

Countdown to go!

Counting down (such as 5, 4, 3, 2 ,1, or 3, 2, 1, go!) focusses attention – rather like 'starters orders' for running a race.

Keep it the same

Undertake the actions on your list the same way every day for at least two weeks, or until they become an unconscious habit.

Build a daily routine

If feasible, study at the same time each day until you establish good study habits.

Create your own study cues

Choose one or more from the following list or add your own.

- Always starting at the same time, such as after dinner, after a walk, after a phone call home, etc.
- After a short mindfulness meditation to settle my thoughts
- Listening to a particular playlist
- Using the same pen
- Switching off social media
- Having a coffee ready on the desk
- Arranging a section of the desk in a particular way
- Positioning a chair ready for study
- Switching on the study lamp
- Putting a sharpened pencil down onto a clean page, ready for notes
- Opening to the right page
- Walking round the room, then sitting down
- Counting down to 'go!'
- Making a 'one-minute plan' of what I am going to do in the next hour
- Performing a 'speed task' (Way 18)
- Putting on glasses
- Taking a sip of water
- Reading an affirmation or a 'message to self'

Other suggestions:

My study cues

1.

2.

3.

4.

5.

6.

Why these would work for me ...

22

Visualise it

See the details with your mind's eye

How does this help?

It requires strong motivation to sit down to study nearly every day for months and years – even if you have clear reasons for doing it. It helps if you can form strong mental images to inspire and guide you along the way. One image might be sufficient. Even better, create several strong images that you can run through as a film or video in your mind's eye. Become immersed in these, as if they were a virtual reality experience. Notice the details. Who else is there? What exactly are you doing? What emotions do you feel? What can you see around you? What do you say to yourself?

Considering your responses

If you have only a vague sense of how you will go about a task or how completing it contributes to your end-goals, visualisation can help. Use a good plan or schedule to help see your route from A–B, or an image of the future to spur motivation. The more details, the better this works.

 See also Ways 20, 21, 39

 Do I ...?

1. Do I use clear mental images to motivate myself to action?

   Yes   **No**

2. Do I feel vague about how I will achieve what I want to do?

   Yes   **No**

3. Do I visualise different stages in the processes I need to follow?

   Yes   **No**

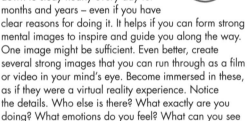 **Find out more**

www.wikihow.com/visualize

To do. I will ...

Picture the outcomes and the journey there!

Picture the route

Run your mental video, from start to finish, of how you will get to the endpoint of your task or course. Write this down in detail to help you visualise.

Picture the first step

What is the first step? What exactly are you doing? When does this take place?

Picture the endpoint

Imagine completing the task. What is the final step? What will be the outcome? What will you be doing and where? When will this be? What will it feel like?

Picture the consequences

... of not getting things done. What might it prevent you from doing? Visualise where you are, and what you will be doing as a result.

Picture positive impacts

Visualise scenarios that can arise from getting the task done. What might it mean for your assignment, course, skills, confidence, self-esteem, job choices, future study, future income, etc.? Run a mental video of relevant scenarios: how do you look, act, react, feel when you gain those benefits?

23 Don't spare your spare minutes!

Make effective use of short spells of time

How does this help?

Across the week, term and year, spare minutes can add up to a considerable amount of unused time. Typically, such times include queuing, waiting for transport, waiting on other people, times between scheduled events, or drifting into spending more time watching videos or TV, playing games, using social media or chatting than you intended. There are many tasks that fit into a spare minute or two – such as a quick browse of a topic coming up in class, testing out a new study app, preparing questions for an upcoming tutorial or class, or viewing hard-to-remember course material. Use spare moments to accomplish more and to keep larger time blocks free for longer tasks.

Considering your responses

If you haven't yet given serious consideration to those passing moments in your week, you could have a fantastic resource to tap into. They are especially good for learning facts and figures without pressure.

 See also Ways 29, 32, 35, 46

 Do I ...?

1. Do I have spare moments I could use for short study bursts?
   Yes   **No**

2. Do I have useful things ready to do when such moments arise?
   Yes   **No**

3. Do I make best use of spare time?
   Yes   **No**

 To do. I will ...

Make the minutes matter!

Spot the opportunities

Become more aware of typical times in your week when you have time you could use more productively.

Look for bankable time

If you can fit essential tasks into spare moments, you could 'bank' that time for rewards and favourite activities later on (see Way 32).

Make a list

… of things you could do in spare moments for a few days ahead.

Retain useful downtime

Downtime is also important for well-being and health (see Way 16) – so don't use up all 'spare time' in study.

Have tasks prepared

Create a set of short tasks to fit into short moments. Decide at the start of the day which you will use.

Carry flashcards

If you find you have unexpected spare time, use these to review facts, figures, charts and diagrams that help with your course. Be well prepared for tests and exams and sound smarter in class.

24

Make great lists

See it all at a glance

How does this help?

Lists are great for staying organised and reminding us of what we need to do. Poor list-making strategies waste time. Over-long lists can be overwhelming, and poorly organised lists can leave us feeling ineffective. Used the right way, lists help to get things done on time, and at the best time. They reduce mental clutter, helping us to relax. We can let go of information we were holding in mind, knowing it is safely captured in a list. Seeing everything in a single organised list provides an overview of the various demands on our time, so we can decide and plan more effectively.

Considering your responses

If you forget things easily or have a lot to remember, lists can ease the pressure. Write them quickly so they don't become a way of avoiding tasks. Make them attractive and easy to use, so that you want to keep using them during the day.

 Do I ...?

1. Do I forget things I meant to do?

   Yes ☐ No ☐

2. Do I make lists and forget them?

   Yes ☐ No ☐

3. Do I feel overwhelmed by my lists?

   Yes ☐ No ☐

4. Do I use my lists effectively?

   Yes ☐ No ☐

 Find out more

www.themuse.com/advice/8-expertbacked-secrets-to-making-the-perfect-todo-list

 To do. I will ...

 See also Ways 15, 20, 23, 34, 44

Keep your list live

Make a 'to-do' list at night

Use it to prepare for the next day.

Clip into your diary/planner

... for each day, so it is always easy to find and see.

Check and update regularly

When you get up, before leaving home, between classes, etc.

Sort items

Sort into actions for today, this week, and longer term. Relocate items that are not 'to-do' actions.

Adapt your list style

... to suit you – such as one long list, or shorter, themed lists.

Make long lists user-friendly

Write lists that are see-at-a-glance and legible. Highlight essential tasks. Flag things that can be left for another day if needed.

Sequence your lists

Number items in the best order for getting things done depending on priorities and where you will be.

Keep them to hand

... to check and update easily.

Focus on one item at a time

... so you don't get overwhelmed by the length of your list.

Enjoy checking items off

... knowing they are completed.

Refresh

Rewrite if hard to read or out of date. Remove things you will never get around to doing.

25 Make study appointments with yourself

And don't be late!

How does this help?

If you don't respect your study time, especially time needed for independent study, it can be wasted and lost all too easily. Don't allow other things to take over study time. Write study tasks into your diary as a series of appointments. Respect these as you would any other appointments that are important to you, such as job interviews, seeing the dentist or your tutor. Ideally, make at least one appointment a day for study outside of formal class time. Prepare for it. Be there on time. Stay focussed.

Considering your responses

If you struggle to make time for independent study, you could benefit from treating your designated study time in a more formal way. Appointments are one way of doing this. These can be especially helpful if your study lacks a sense of urgency, such as when there isn't an exam to sit or assignment to submit in the near future.

 See also Ways 6, 12, 29, 36, 43

 Do I ...?

1. Do I always have enough time for autonomous (independent) study?

   Yes ☐ No ☐

2. Do I respect study time as I would any other formal appointment?

   Yes ☐ No ☐

3. Do I always keep to the time I have put aside for autonomous study?

   Yes ☐ No ☐

 To do. I will ...

Honour your study appointments

Same start time every day

Make an appointment in your diary for some study every day. You may have more time available some days than others but, if you can, start at the same time.

Plan for the time you need

Nobody likes to feel that they were rushed through an appointment. It feels like a lack of respect. Calculate how much time you need to spend on study over several days, and plan that into your diary so it doesn't feel rushed.

Be punctual

Punctuality is a sign of respect. Respect your study by starting all sessions at the time you had planned. Start exactly on schedule – not a minute late.

Keep your appointments

If you have class, work or family commitments, organise your study appointments around these, at times when you are likely to be able to keep them. Make sure you turn up!

Don't let anyone interrupt

You wouldn't normally expect important appointments to be interrupted, so respect study appointments in a similar way.

26

Organise notes and information

Organisation = time

How does this help?

Being a student involves managing a vast amount of information. You can save, or waste, a significant amount of time depending on how quickly you can find stored material when you need it. It isn't always immediately apparent what you will need later in the course or for an assignment, so it is easy to accumulate much more information than you need. Manage this by being organised in the way you write, label and store information as you go along.[17] Sort and reorganise information regularly. It will also help you to understand how course material connects up and to remember it.

Considering your responses

If you waste time retrieving information, searching through notes and wondering where you found information originally, then better note-making and information management can save you time – for your time bank! (See Way 32.)

 Do I ...?

1. Do I waste time hunting for material that I know I have used or noted before?

Yes **No**

2. Do I re-organise notes regularly?

Yes **No**

3. Do I keep an accurate record of the sources of information I read and note?

Yes **No**

 Find out more

The Study Skills Handbook, Cottrell (2019)[17]

 To do. I will ...

 See also Ways 31, 32, 41, 46

Find it fast!

Name it – for easy searching

Whether using files, folders, boxes, or emails, give them names, labels or subject lines that let you know precisely what each contains and how it differs to similar items.

Store updated copies

… of draft assignments and electronic notes in the cloud. Save time having to redo lost work!

Throw stuff away

… once you finish with it. Have a good clear-out regularly.

Cross-reference

If material could be useful for several assignments or answers, write it once and refer across to this, as relevant, in other sets of notes or in outline plans.

Use theme colours

… for binders, notebooks, highlighting, underlining, quotes for each subject, class or topic. It helps you find things at speed.

Keep details of sources

Include the page number so you can look things up quickly if you need to, such as for references.

Make a contents list

Keep a list of where to find information you might lose otherwise.

Colour-code

Use different colours for quotations and anything not in your own words: it saves time going back to sources to check you haven't plagiarised them in assignments.

27

Break the tedium!

Keep your study fresh and meaningful

How does this help?

If you feel bored, you can't use time effectively. Boredom generally means that you haven't established a personal connection with the task. If it really matters to you, it won't be boring. If there isn't an obvious connection, then make one. Consider, for example, the personal consequences of doing, or not doing the task, or how you could apply the information you cover. Check whether you might just be hungry, thirsty, tired or in need of a change of scene. If you have a strong daily study routine, allow yourself to break it at times – to bring a fresh perspective and re-energise your study.

Considering your responses

If you are easily bored or distracted when studying, then don't just suffer through it or waste time drifting off onto other things. Plan your time smartly, giving thought to what will make each study task more interesting for you. Don't assume you can't make it interesting. Vary your use of time with short, timed tasks so there isn't time to get bored.

 See also Ways 18, 20, 32, 34, 39

 Do I ...?

1. Do I get bored studying?

Yes **No**

2. Do I find I read the same material over and over without taking it in?

Yes **No**

3. Do I get distracted easily from study?

Yes **No**

 Find out more

The Study Skills Handbook, Cottrell (2019)[17]

 To do. I will ...

Vary your time!

Connect to the task

What is the benefit to you in completing it? What will you learn? How could it be of use later? Why is it important to anyone else? How would you make it interesting to others?

Vary your daily routine

Plan a different day to yesterday. Take a different route around campus. Eat somewhere new. Sit in a different seat in the library.

Take breaks

When your attention wanes, take a 3-minute break to stretch, or work on a different aspect of the task.

Find food for thought

Don't just go through the motions of learning or 'covering the information' such as by reading or listening passively. Be active in questioning the material, looking for significance and linking ideas.

Build in some speed-tasking

It adds a sense of urgency that helps reduce boredom (see Way 18).

Break up long sessions

Plan many short tasks. Vary the sequence of these in a way logical to the overall task, such as jotting down questions, reading, making notes, checking data, listening to a talk, thinking, planning or writing a paragraph, proofreading, etc.

28

Focus on one task at a time

Stick to what you start

How does this help?

Every time you move from one task to another, even for a split second, your brain switches off from the first task, and has to work harder to refocus afterwards.[33] If you are doing two or more things at once, the brain is working harder so becomes tired and stressed faster. Students who 'multi-task' lose blocks of time without realising it. Maintaining focus in class and meetings saves time later: you don't need to spend as much time catching up and sorting out confusion arising from missed information.

Considering your responses

If your responses suggest that you are dividing your attention, your brain is task-switching at speed. Studies show that even people who think they are good at multi-tasking are much less effective than those who focus on one task at a time.[34] You use time more effectively if you can build your ability to concentrate for longer.

 See also Ways 4, 27, 34, 46

 Do I ...?

1. Do I tend to hop around between tasks?

   Yes   **No**

2. Do I think I am good at multi-tasking?

   Yes   **No**

3. Do I keep an eye on messages and media whilst studying?

   Yes   **No**

 Find out more

Mindfulness for Students, Cottrell (2018)[16]

 To do. I will ...

Give your undivided attention

Don't flit between tasks

Once you begin a task, keep going until you finish. You get more done if you don't have to keep restarting tasks after shifting attention.

Value the moment

Giving tasks your full attention helps you to gain more from each moment. You learn more and gain more satisfaction from study.

Use undivided attention

Focus on each task until completed. If you need to, check media and messages before moving onto your next task.

Build your attention span

Learn and use mindfulness techniques to increase your ability to focus whilst studying.[16]

Focus in class

Follow what is being said. You won't need to spend time later on checking whether you missed anything. You also won't lose out on useful emphases, tips and details.

Sequence tasks well

Be clear in your own mind that you are working on the most important task, so you are less distracted by other things that are queuing.

29 Know where your time goes!

Gain insights into your own use of time

? Do I ...?

1. Do I know how much of my time is spent on things I didn't plan to do?

   Yes ☐ No ☐

2. Do I know how much of my time I spend on activities I don't really value later?

   Yes ☐ No ☐

How does this help?

We tend to over-estimate our efficiency in using time. Keeping a log for a few days can provide you with insights into where exactly all that time goes. You can then decide whether you want to continue to spend time in that way or make some changes. Monitoring your time shows whether you are more efficient at certain tasks at different times of the day or week. It also shows whether you have enough time for rest, chatting and fun too. It can feel annoying to log everything down, but it is worth it if you want a really accurate sense of your actual time use.

Considering your responses

If you aren't sure how and where your time gets wasted, you could benefit from keeping a time log for a few days. Just make a few columns in a notebook (as opposite) so it is easy to jot items down quickly. Add up your time use and decide where you could save time.

ⓘ Find out more

The Study Skills Handbook, Cottrell (2019)[17]

To do. I will ...

See also Ways 4, 26, 32

Keep a time log

Time your activity and rate it **0–5** (5 being the best use of time at that point).
*Add details that help you to assess your use of time accurately.

Time	Activity	Duration?	Planned?	Best use of time?
10.00	Chat with Tom	25 mins	No	0
10.30	*10 a.m. lecture	25 mins	Yes	4
10.45	Checked phone	3 mins	No	1
11.05	Went for coffee	55 mins	20 mins*	2
12.02	Study in library	8 mins	Yes	4
12.10	Used social media	6 mins	No	1
12.16	Read article	12 mins	No	5

Reflect on your time use

1. Work out how much time in the week is spent on different kinds of task (study, chat, games, time with friends, etc.). Decide if that is in line with where you consider your time would be spent best.

2. Roughly what proportion of your time use do you rate 0–3?

3. How often was your focus interrupted (by you/others)?

4. What is the overall effect of the way you spend time?

5. What insights does this provide about how to use your time better?

30 Manage clustered deadlines

Ease pressure on assignment submission deadlines

? Do I ...?

1. Do I get stressed when deadlines cluster together in the diary?

   Yes ☐ **No** ☐

2. Do I worry that I won't be able to complete two items for the same day?

   Yes ☐ **No** ☐

3. Do I moan if I have more than one exam or assignment close together?

   Yes ☐ **No** ☐

How does this help?

Students often complain that, like buses, there are no serious deadlines for a while, then several come at once. You might need to submit two assignments within a few hours of each other or sit two exams on the same day. Whilst this is worrying if you leave everything to the last minute, it can mean you have more choice about how to distribute your study time. Instead of worrying that the deadlines are close together, devise a schedule to spread the workload for each one over several weeks – it is better for learning and recall, and reduces stress.

Considering your responses

If you worry about deadlines and exams clustering around the same date, then ease your stress through good forward planning. It takes self-discipline but is worth it for better grades and happier study.

ⓘ Find out more

The Exam Skills Handbook, Cottrell (2012)[31] and *The Study Skills Handbook*, Cottrell (2019)[17]

To do. I will ...

See also Ways 12, 17, 42, 49

Avoid the panic!

Decide it isn't a problem

Take the approach that you have been given additional time to hand in one of the assignments – if they were on different dates, you would probably have been given less time for one of them.

Use long-term revision

Recall will be better if you start revision earlier. See Way 42.

Make a good schedule

Plan out exactly when you will undertake the various tasks required for each assignment.

Set your own deadlines

If two deadlines fall on the same day, set your own deadlines for completing one early.

Register the skill!

Achieving tight deadlines is typical in graduate jobs, so appreciate the practice. Note down the skills you are developing. Managing several assignments or exams at once might make it easier to cope with future work scenarios!

Build in contingency time

Things don't always go as planned: you might get ill, have an unexpected event to attend or need to wait for a book. Leave time to get back on track if needed.

31 Create time through space management

Find time and calm, through decluttering your space

 Do I ...?

1. Do I work in chaos?
   Yes ☐ No ☐

2. Do I waste time looking for things?
   Yes ☐ No ☐

3. Do I feel overwhelmed by my desk?
   Yes ☐ No ☐

How does this help?

A cluttered space adds to mental clutter, and leads to inefficiencies and wasted time. Things get lost. It takes longer to find things. It distracts. It leads to mistakes. It causes the brain to work harder and tire faster. A cluttered room or desk sends signals to the brain that it has to expend a lot of energy leading it to feel pressurised and demotivated. Studies suggest people waste over two and a half days a year just looking for misplaced items.[35] However, a messy environment can release creativity, so a cluttered area can be useful.[36]

 Find out more

www.independent.co.uk/life-style/lost-found-property-keys-how-to-find-study-university-aberdeen-clutter-a7593331.html[37]

Considering your responses

If you are discouraged, overwhelmed or just weary with the results of a messy desk or room, then you know it's time for a tidy-up. If a totally clear desk policy doesn't suit you, at least make your study space look welcoming. Put most of the clutter where you can't see it.

 To do. I will ...

 See also Ways 15, 26, 29, 44

Clear desk – clear mind

Keep your desk clear

- Sort and clear most things away when you finish study.

- Make your desk inviting for study, depending on whether you need to generate ideas or clarify your thoughts.

Declutter regularly

Get rid of things you don't need. If you haven't time to sort everything, put clutter out of sight. Set a time in your diary to sort it out later.

Everything in its place

Be consistent in where you keep things. Put them back after use. You save time by automatically going to the right place.

One place to look!

Keep all small easy-to-lose items together in one place in your room and in a small zipped bag for items you carry around in the day.

Check cluttered space first

If you lose an item, research suggests it is most likely to be in a messy area. It saves time to check there rather than cleared spaces.[37]

32

Create a time bank

Gain the benefits of using time more efficiently

Do I ...?

1. Do I plan how to use time efficiently?

   Yes ☐ **No** ☐

2. Do I need motivation to 'save' time?

   Yes ☐ **No** ☐

3. Do I run out of time for study assignments and/or for other activities?

   Yes ☐ **No** ☐

How does this help?

Some students settle down to study quickly. They take regular breaks to recharge the brain, and stay focussed when studying, using time effectively. Others take a long time to settle or waste time across the day. Later on, they find they are under pressure to complete assignments and cannot fit in social life, rest and other commitments. Creating a 'time bank' can bring an element of fun to time-efficiency whilst serving the serious purposes of helping you to use time well. You just need to 'bank' time you save through good time management.

Considering your responses

If you are not generally very conscious about time efficiency and need more time to do everything you would like to do in the day, then a 'time bank' might help. It can make you more aware of whether you are really using time in the way you want. Just follow the steps opposite!

See also Ways 13, 29, 35, 46

To do. I will ...

Enjoy the time saved

Find time to save
Become aware of where you waste time unnecessarily (see Way 29).

Log minutes saved
Keep a record of the time you save through using time more efficiently. Log time you waste too! The time you save, on balance, is your 'time bank' – to spend as you choose!

Monitor your log
… to keep you focussed.

Set time-saving goals
… such as a minimum number of minutes to save each week.

Make genuine savings
Don't cut corners such as rushing work or missing essential steps just to add to your time bank.

Decide where to spend it
… on social activity, a fun day out, a sleep-in when you might otherwise have had to study.

Map it into your diary
Allocate blocks of time in your diary to spend the time you save. If you save enough time in your log, you gain the reward of that time to spend as you wish.

Appreciate it!
Congratulate yourself on making time! Enjoy spending it!

33

Get a time cheerleader!

Gain support from others!

How does this help?

We are more likely to complete what we need to do and achieve our goals if we tell others about our ambitions. If you struggle to fulfil your best intentions with respect to time management, then get some help from family, friends or a mentor that you trust. Tell them exactly what you want them to do and when. This could be to cheer you on to the next task with a well-timed text or to congratulate you when you complete an important stage of an assignment. Use whatever works for you! Make it a condition that you commit to do whatever you arrange with your cheerleader. Report back honestly to them when you do.

Considering your responses

If you feel you would benefit from a time-management cheerleader, and have someone you trust, then talk this through with them. Agree a realistic plan. Your institution's mentoring scheme might also help.

 See also Ways 4, 15, 21, 37

 Do I ...?

1. Do I need support to manage time?

   Yes ☐ No ☐

2. Do I have someone I trust to encourage me in the ways I need?

   Yes ☐ No ☐

3. Do I think I would respond well to having a time-management cheerleader?

   Yes ☐ No ☐

 To do. I will ...

Be a great time team!

Choose the right person(s)

Choose one or more people who will be happy to help and encourage you in the way you need. It could be another student for whom you act as cheerleader in return.

Be clear about what you need

Agree with your cheerleader(s) precisely what they will do.

Report back

Tell your cheerleader(s) what happened and what helped.

Review what didn't work

Decide what needs to change.

Be realistic

Don't ask them to phone you in the middle of the night to see if you are still working on your assignment.

Celebrate together

When your task, assignment or project is complete, let your cheerleader know. Thank them! Have a coffee or meal to celebrate!

34

Plan out each study session

Know your focus and next task

How does this help?

Managing independent study time is a major challenge. It is easier to focus when an exam or assignment submission date is imminent, but you need to be efficient and effective using time even when there isn't an immediate deadline. This is a good skill to acquire – not just for study but also for working life. Success often depends on work undertaken well ahead of deadlines. In effect, you have to create your own deadlines for the short term. A good way of doing this is to be clear about what to accomplish during each day and study session. This helps you to focus so each step is accomplished in the best order – on time.

Considering your responses

If you tend to have vague daily study goals such as 'working on my assignment', then provide your day and study sessions with a sharper focus. Be specific about what you will complete each day and for each time you sit down to study.

 **See also** Ways 4, 18, 36, 39

 Do I ...?

1. Do I sit down to study with a clear idea of what I want to achieve that session?

   Yes ☐ No ☐

2. Do I make a list of tasks that I need to complete to achieve that goal?

   Yes ☐ No ☐

3. Do I plan study for the hour ahead?

   Yes ☐ No ☐

 To do. I will …

Work to daily goals

Decide ✔ what would be useful for you to follow up.

Set study goals for the day
In your diary, jot down what you intend to achieve. What will you complete by the end of the day?

Use hourly study sessions
Break your day into study sessions of around an hour. Plan in short breaks if you find these useful. If several sessions follow each other, make sure you take some breaks.

Find your focus
Using your overall plan for the day, decide a focus for the next 1–2 hours.

Use a one-minute plan
Don't get distracted into spending the whole session planning it. Jot down a quick 'to-do' list for the next hour or two, allocating time to each item. Number them in the best order for completing them.

Plan each study session
Get into the habit of making a one-minute plan each time you sit down to study. It focusses you and reminds you to get on with it.

Your plan got disrupted?
Don't waste time despairing! Do a rapid update and get focussed on the next item on your list.

Keep it varied
Vary tasks to avoid boredom.

Calm your thoughts first
… with a walk, short mindfulness meditation or relaxation exercise.[16]

35 Utilise 'surround time' for classes

Gain full value from time spent in class

 Do I ...?

1. Do I focus on what is said in class?

   Yes ☐ No ☐

2. Do I take great notes in class?

   Yes ☐ No ☐

3. Do I follow up on questions, gaps, points of interest etc. after class?

   Yes ☐ No ☐

How does this help?

Time spent in class, whether in lectures, labs, seminars, tutorials, workshops or with guest speakers, constitutes an important part of a course. Class time tends to be intense, covering a lot of new concepts using specialist terminology. You need to focus for a relatively long time, absorb what is being said, be alert to what is relevant, and select and note material whilst still listening. That is demanding. Often, students' attention drifts so they miss material without realising. With good preparation and follow-up, and using the time that surrounds the class, it is easier to understand, concentrate and gain value from it.

Considering your responses

You learn more if you devote a few minutes in advance to familiarise yourself with the material. Jot down a few questions to guide your attention in class. Afterwards, read through your notes to check they make sense. Follow up on any gaps and unanswered questions straightaway. This reinforces learning, understanding and memory recall.

 Find out more

The Study Skills Handbook, Cottrell (2019)[17]

 To do. I will …

 See also Ways 18, 21, 38, 43

Prepare and follow up

Browse ahead
Get a feel for the material in advance, so it is familiar in class. You will follow what is said more easily and feel more confident.

Note names, facts, concepts
You are more likely to spot these in the lecture if you have already noted them, and less likely to miss other essential information if you don't need to note them in class.

Formulate questions
Jot down questions about issues that interest you or that you hope the lecture will clarify. Listen out for answers during the class.

Follow up
... on anything that caught your interest, that could be useful for assignments, work or exams, or that you didn't fully understand.

Read through your notes
Read through your notes after class. If these are incomplete, ask others about material you missed or look it up.

36 Plan your week

Schedule a balanced week for yourself

 Do I ...?

1. Do I plan out each week?

   Yes [ ] **No** [ ]

2. Do I look ahead in my schedule to see what I could put into action well in advance?

   Yes [ ] **No** [ ]

3. Do I plan variety, balance and interest across each week?

   Yes [ ] **No** [ ]

How does this help?

A week is a useful and manageable period for organising time and viewing it at a glance. As class schedules are usually the same for at least a term or semester, it makes sense to plan time around classes. Planning your week helps you to activate your 'time power' (see Way 1) and to be more confident about getting essential tasks done. It also enables you to consider all of your needs and interests, and to experience a more balanced week. Reviewing your priorities weekly helps to focus the mind and encourage action. Don't plan every minute: leave time to fit in the unexpected, so it is easier to move things around if needed.

Considering your responses

If you don't currently plan your week well, consider making this a new habit. It doesn't need to take long, yet it can bring great benefits: clarity about what you are doing, reassurance that you will cover essential tasks, confidence, reduced stress and an overall better experience as a student.

 See also Ways 1, 12, 14, 25, 44

 Find out more

The Macmillan Student Planner, Cottrell (updated annually)[21]

 To do. I will ...

No nasty surprises!

Set time for weekly planning
Create a routine of taking 15–30 minutes to plan the week ahead.

Browse your schedule
Check at least 2–4 weeks ahead. Identify things to set in motion this week – to ease pressures later and to be well prepared in upcoming weeks.

List and prioritise
… things you must, and would like to, do this week. Plan the 'must do' items into your diary first, in pencil. Work out which other items on your list can be fitted in, and where. What can be pencilled into future weeks?

Plan for balance and variety
Create a week that contains fun, interest, social life, and activities to support health, well-being and personal development – and study!

Use a week to view diary
… so you can see your week at a glance wherever you are.[21]

Be flexible
Your weekly plan is a guide – it doesn't need to be set in stone. If you do change the plan, pause to work out where moved items will fit. Don't be vague about where you will fit in anything essential.

Plan enough time for treats
… so you don't try to take these when you have other priorities!

37

Be time-collaborative

Use the power of the group

How does this help?

Working collaboratively helps you to gain more from your study time. Social learning can be fun, engaging your interests and energies for longer. Doing tasks for the group can spur you to get things done which you might not if just for yourself. There are many tasks you can share as a student. These include reviewing class notes, searching out and sharing books and online resources, comparing study apps, discussing course theories, checking understanding of course material, testing for facts and figures, etc. When sharing, always make sure you work within the regulations. Don't share drafts or completed assignments before everyone's work has been graded.

Considering your responses

Grasp opportunities to build team skills. You can share study-related tasks, or everyday living tasks, with just one person, one team, or diverse teams. If you are not sure of the rules for sharing out tasks at your institution, find these out first.

 See also Ways 32, 33, 38, 49

 Do I ...?

1. Do I know what kind of collaborative work is allowed on my course?

   Yes **No**

2. Do I know what is prohibited?

   Yes **No**

3. Do I work well in a team?

   Yes **No**

 Find out more

The Study Skills Handbook, Cottrell (2019)[17]

 To do. I will ...

Share creatively as part of a great team

Choose your 'team' wisely
Share with people you trust so everyone contributes fairly.

Choose what you share
Find out which study-related tasks can be shared legitimately. You can share non-study tasks too, from car-sharing and food shopping, picking up laundry or library books, to dog walking or babysitting for students with children.

Gain team-working skills
Collaboration develops a range of attributes useful for working life. You can gain insights into how reliable you are as a team member and the roles that suit you best. You can learn to allocate work fairly and communicate effectively as a team.

Debate course material
Discussing course material with others is a good way of learning it. It is easier to remember material when different points of view are being debated within the group.

38

Be there!

Gain a reputation for punctuality and attendance

How does this help?

Being present and punctual adds to your confidence, reduces stress and means you gain the full benefit of the class or meeting – saving you time later. It sends a positive message that you are reliable and respect other people and their time. It shows tutors you are serious about your study, which helps if something were to go wrong. It can also make the difference when selections are made for teams, study groups, prizes, mentoring or leadership roles. In addition, employers value attendance and punctuality: your tutor might be asked to comment on these if employers ask the university to write a job reference for you.

Considering your responses

If you could improve your attendance and punctuality, consider the impression you are making. Be aware of how it could affect you and others and what you miss when you are just not there. Plan and time things well so that you make a habit of turning up and being punctual.

 See also Ways 9, 15, 23, 37, 49

 Do I ...?

1. Do I always turn up for class?

Yes ☐ No ☐

2. Do I always arrive on time when meeting people and for class?

Yes ☐ No ☐

3. Do I tend to sneak away early from class or meetings?

Yes ☐ No ☐

 Find out more

The Macmillan Student Planner, Cottrell (updated annually)[21]

 To do. I will ...

Respect others' time as well as your own

Be a team player

Show respect to others: assume your punctuality and presence makes a difference to their plans, learning and experience of the day.

Know what's coming up

Record all classes, meetings and events into your diary, with time and location. Check your planner regularly.[21]

Plan to arrive early

Check your route, transport and travel times. Leave sufficient time to arrive at least 5 minutes early even if transport is disrupted.

Don't get waylaid

Avoid unscheduled shopping, chats and changes of plan – or leave sufficient time to cover these.

Early start?

If you have the choice of arriving much earlier or just a few minutes late, see if you can negotiate a planned late arrival. Otherwise, be on time even if this means getting up very early. Plan how you will use the time if you arrive early.

Don't leave class early

Once in class, make it worthwhile. Stay focussed from start to finish and don't sneak out early. You benefit – and it keeps your tutors on your side.

39 Spell out your next move

Expect the unexpected!

 Do I ...?

1. Do I get distracted when studying?

   Yes ☐ **No** ☐

2. Does my mind drift when studying?

   Yes ☐ **No** ☐

3. Do I waste time between tasks?

   Yes ☐ **No** ☐

4. Do I find it hard to settle to study?

   Yes ☐ **No** ☐

How does this help?

Typically, we don't mean to get distracted by time-wasting activities. They catch us off guard and draw us in. We realise after the event that time we intended for an activity has been dissipated on other things. Studies show that we use time more effectively if we plan what we will do in the event of various circumstances arising.[38] We can handle interruptions, distractions and procrastination more easily if we set out our intentions clearly. The more specific we are, the better this works: 'If my friends suggest we meet up, I will say no'. 'When I finish reading this part, I will make notes about it then browse the rest of the chapter'.

Considering your responses

If you tend to get drawn easily into distractions from your original goal for the day or for study sessions, then take a couple of minutes to clarify what you intend will happen and what your responses will be to anything that could disrupt this. It is easier to make such decisions in advance.

 See also Ways 4, 15, 29, 34, 46

 To do. I will ...

Plan your response

Clarify your intention

What exactly do you want to do with your time over the next hour/for the evening, etc.? (See Ways 15 and 34.)

Spot likely scenarios

Consider what might distract you into time-wasting during the next hour or so. 'What if this person phones?' or 'What if I get a lot of messages?'

Decide on a precise response

'If this happens I am going to do X' and 'I will say X'. 'I will check my messages between 10 and 10.15. Then I will start doing ...'

Plan your transitions

Decide what you will do when you have finished a task or a break: 'When I finish making notes on this chapter, I will draft an outline plan for my essay'.

Protect your week

Plan your week and check your diary before agreeing to activities that will divert you from what you need to do.

40

Put in sufficient effective study hours

Spend the right time on task

How does this help?

When courses are designed, it is assumed that students will spend a minimum number of hours in order to pass. Typically, a full-time course is the broad equivalent of a full-time job of around 35 hours a week. The time you will need to spend depends on a number of factors, such as course difficulty, your familiarity with the material and how well you concentrate. If you don't study effectively for the expected number of hours, it is unlikely you will do well. Find out how your tutors expect students to distribute study time on different kinds of activity across the course. Compare that with your own use.

Considering your responses

If you are not aware of how many hours you are meant to study for your course, or how that compares to your own time use, take the steps opposite. Be aware that designated hours are based on an 'average' student, so you might need to study less – or more!

 See also Ways 11, 29, 45, 46

 Do I ...?

1. Do I know how many hours I am expected to study each week, on average?

   Yes ☐ **No** ☐

2. Do I know how many hours I actually study?

   Yes ☐ **No** ☐

3. Do I know how many of those hours I spend focussed on the study task?

   Yes ☐ **No** ☐

 Find out more

The Study Skills Handbook, Cottrell (2019)[17]

 To do. I will ...

Compare your effective study hours against course time requirements

Decide ✔ what would be useful for you to follow up.

Know the overall time requirements for the course

- The total expected study hours for each level of study

- For attendance in class

Check time expectations

- For each assignment

- For each week during terms or semesters

- For study in vacations

- For distributing study hours across different kinds of task such as time in class, reading, researching, writing, thinking, etc.

Add up the hours

- ... that you put aside for study each week

- ... that you actually study each week

- ... that you are truly focussed on relevant study tasks

- ... on study-related activity that isn't really needed

Assess your needs

Work out whether you can achieve the grades and other outcomes you want from your course using fewer effective study hours than would normally be required – or whether you might need to put in additional hours.

41

Use focussed reading strategies

Sharpen higher reading skills

How does this help?

Higher level study usually involves a great deal of reading. You are expected to read widely to understand your subject from varied perspectives and to be up to date on the latest issues and research. At some point, most students struggle to fit in the required reading. This can be stressful and undermine confidence. Because academic reading is demanding, if the brain tires or loses focus, it can seem as if the time spent reading is both wasted and slipping away. Using focussed reading approaches puts you more in control of reading time. You concentrate for longer and on the most relevant material.

Considering your responses

If you read things that aren't really relevant, make more notes when reading than you can ever use or recall, or find you drift off when reading, then you are wasting valuable time. You could benefit from taking a more active, directed approach to your reading.[17]

 See also Ways 18, 21, 26, 28

 Do I ...?

1. Do I stay focussed when reading?

   Yes ☐ No ☐

2. Do I waste time when reading?

   Yes ☐ No ☐

3. Do I use most of what I read?

   Yes ☐ No ☐

4. Do I make helpful notes about what I read?

   Yes ☐ No ☐

 Find out more

The Study Skills Handbook, Cottrell (2019)[17]

 To do. I will ...

Direct your reading

Formulate questions
... to steer your reading. These help you to spot the information you need and to focus on relevant material.

Mix it up!
Alternate reading with related study tasks, such as selecting the most relevant points to note, summing up theories, arguments or evidence in your own words, searches inspired by your reading, or planning out a paragraph based on your reading.

Be selective
Work out as precisely as you can the material you will need to include in assignment or exam answers, or to fully understand the subject. Use headings in the text, the index, and good browsing to identify the areas where you need to focus for intense reading.

Make notes by hand
This helps you remember information better, saving time when revising. It also reduces the risk of plagiarism.

Avoid duplication
Use good headings for your notes, so you can check back over these before reading texts that cover similar material. Add to your notes only if needed, rather than writing out similar material all over again.

42 Phase your revision over time

Stage your revision over many weeks

Do I …?

1. Do I leave revision until the last minute?

   Yes ☐ No ☐

2. Do I ignore a lot of material as I don't have time to learn it?

   Yes ☐ No ☐

3. Do I forget details when in exams?

   Yes ☐ No ☐

How does this help?

Your brain needs time to revise well: to absorb material, make sense of it, make connections and lay down memories so that you can recall it easily and with relatively high certainty when needed. There is usually a significant amount to remember for exams, which puts strain on available brain resources. It helps if you don't revise everything at once. That usually means starting to review and learn material early on. This provides multiple benefits, such as having time to cover all the topics you need, being able to space revision on difficult topics which helps recall, leaving time to revise material covered at the end of the course, and easing the pressure just before exams.

 Find out more

The Exam Skills Handbook, Cottrell (2012)[31]

Considering your responses

If you don't already phase your revision over time, then ease your way into exams. Reduce pressure on yourself whilst making better opportunities to learn and apply the material. As a first step, draw up a revision timetable now.

 To do. I will …

 See also Ways 7, 10, 23, 48

Give your brain time to learn it!

Help your autopilot

Start early in learning facts and figures such as names, dates, statistical data, lists and formulae. Rehearse these until you can draw upon them on 'autopilot'.

Schedule early revision

List and timetable material you will learn earlier in the year – and plan it into your diary.

Leave time to rework it

... to reorganise and summarise notes, devise mnemonics, and apply material to varied questions.

Gain the sleep effect

Your brain needs to sleep on information in order to process it effectively. Otherwise, it struggles to recall information under pressure. For best revision, don't leave it to the night before or you miss out on the benefit of that sleep effect.

Devise a revision schedule

Plan out when you will revise the various topics for your course – so you aren't caught out having too many to revise in too little time.

Refresh your recall

Go back over material you learned early on to refresh your recall. Read something new on those topics to re-stimulate your interest.

Boost confidence

... and ease stress from knowing you have covered and learned the material and don't need to cram it the night before.

43 Catch up quickly on missed work

Don't fall behind!

How does this help?

Ideally, you would organise your time and work so that you are always one step ahead. However, even with great intentions, events arise that might mean you miss a class, get behind in your work or develop gaps in your understanding. It is difficult to keep going and to feel good about your course if you know you are falling behind. The longer you leave it, the harder it becomes. The work you missed can make it harder to understand other aspects of the course, adding to study problems. You feel much more in control if you make time straightaway to catch up.

Considering your responses

If you have low motivation for speedy 'catch-up', that is not unusual. Allow yourself the luxury of not being in that position for long – by planning in catch-up time as soon as you know you need it.

 Do I ...?

1. Do I make time to catch up on missed classes during that same week?

   Yes ☐ **No** ☐

2. Do I remember all the things I intend to catch up on?

   Yes ☐ **No** ☐

3. Do I keep putting off catching up on course material I don't fully understand?

   Yes ☐ **No** ☐

 To do. I will ...

 See also Ways 8, 10, 12, 44

Make the time!

Consider ✔ what you need to catch up on now.

- [ ] Missed classes and course-related events

- [ ] Tasks you were meant to complete between classes, but didn't

- [ ] Gaps in your notes from class that you need to fill

- [ ] Things you didn't understand in class and meant to look up

- [ ] Items you meant to read

- [ ] Details you wanted to check

- [ ] Things you rushed first time round (to cover them in sufficient depth)

Other things? List them!

Keep a 'catch up' list
... to remember all the things you meant to follow up.

Don't make excuses
Put into a diary/planner the times you will devote to catch-up. Don't leave it until the end of the course, as that will feel worse and be harder then both to do and to fit in.

Leave catch-up space
Leave some space in your diary each week for the specific purpose of catching up. This is easier than taking time away from planned activities. If you don't then need it, you have extra time to spend as you want!

44

Set yourself reminders

A good reminder means less mental clutter

How does this help?

If you tend to forget things, or are used to other people reminding you, then get into the habit of setting up your own reminders. This is especially important for student life as there are many things to plan in advance so it is easy to forget some. If you have a busy day, or need to break a well-established routine, it is more likely that you will forget something. Set reminders where you know you will see them. If you are especially forgetful, then set them in several places – so you can't miss them!

Considering your responses

If you have a lot to remember, or just forget easily, it makes sense to set yourself strong and hard-to-avoid reminders. It is likely you already do this for some things, but could gain from being systematic in setting more reminders in more places for things you tend to forget or overlook until the last minute.

 See also Ways 9, 15, 17, 24, 33

 Do I ...?

1. Do I have lots to remember?

   Yes ☐ **No** ☐

2. Do I forget to do things I had meant to do during the day?

   Yes ☐ **No** ☐

3. Do I get caught up in what I am doing and forget class or other essentials?

   Yes ☐ **No** ☐

 Find out more

The Macmillan Student Planner, Cottrell (updated annually)[21]

 To do. I will ...

So you can't miss it!

In your diary/planner
Build reminders into your diary as a natural part of your daily routine. Don't just write in the final deadlines. Specify times for starting and completing contributing tasks too.

Visual reminders
For one-off 'urgent for today' reminders, put these on sticky notes on your laptop, diary, your mirror, door, wherever you know you can't miss them. Add it to your screen-saver.

Send yourself a message
Send yourself an email or text message the night before so it is waiting for you when you next check these.

Use an alert or timer
… on your phone, calendar or time-management app.

Ask your cheerleader
If it is really important, ask your cheerleader if they would mind reminding you, too! (See Way 33.)

Or use an app
… such as 'Remember the Milk' or 'Any.do'.
See *The Macmillan Student Planner* for an annually updated list of apps useful for managing time and student life.[21]

45 Avoid the trap of perfectionism

A low mark is better than no mark

How does this help?

It is fine to be ambitious, and to aim for the highest possible grades from beautifully completed work. If you can achieve that in the time available and maintain a healthy balanced life, that is great. If you don't quite make it, then take a reality check. It is not worth risking a capped low mark for late submission because you spent too long perfecting an assignment – or a fail for not submitting at all. Nor is it worth your health and well-being. Push yourself – but not at the expense of everything else. Decide on what is the best you can accomplish for a rounded and healthy experience in the time you have.

Considering your responses

If you know that you submit work late or fall behind with assignments because you want to keep improving them, then perfectionism could be your worst enemy. Work out your best balanced outcome – aim for that.

 See also Ways 8, 12, 18, 34

 Do I ...?

1. Do I spend too long on some tasks and then not finish assignments in time?

   Yes ☐ **No** ☐

2. Do I avoid handing in work because I am never satisfied with it?

   Yes ☐ **No** ☐

3. Do I feel bad if my work isn't perfect?

   Yes ☐ **No** ☐

 To do. I will ...

Balance the rewards

'Perfect' – use as a guide

Set high standards, but don't tie yourself to a perfect outcome that isn't feasible.
You could miss out on good grades or the qualification by trying too hard.

Work to your best outcome

Whilst aiming high, plan your use of time to ensure
that you maintain other important aspects of your life.

Get beyond step 1

Don't spend so long perfecting the first steps that you fall
behind with the rest of an assignment. Set and keep to a schedule.

Submit that assignment!

Get it in on time, even if it is not perfect.
Avoid gaining a low capped mark for late submission.

Gain from submitting work

You might do better than you expect. You gain tutor feedback to use for future
assignments or if you need to re-submit your work.
You also demonstrate commitment and punctuality, which can
work to your favour in future for job references or appeals.

Graduate on time!

... with classmates. Don't get behind by trying for perfection.

46 Cut out study time-wasters

Use study time more efficiently

How does this help?

Time is wasted partly through the obvious distractions and disruptions (see Ways 4 and 29). In addition to these, many students waste time in the way they approach study tasks. A typical indicator of this is when you feel you are working hard but getting nowhere. You might be able to achieve more without working harder. Studies indicate that students who plan well achieve their goals in less time than others.[39] Time is not wasted if it serves a good purpose. Many activities that might appear to be 'time-wasting', such as downtime and even daydreaming and play, are essential to health, learning and memory (see Way 16).

Considering your responses

If you are not getting a good return on the effort you put into study, see opposite for some typical ways that students use time ineffectively when apparently working hard. Observe your study habits and reflect honestly about whether any of these are reducing your study efficiency.

 See also Ways 26, 29, 34, 39

 Do I ...?

1. Do I seem to put a lot of effort into study for too little effect?

   Yes ☐ **No** ☐

2. Do I know where I waste study time?

   Yes ☐ **No** ☐

3. Do I need to use study time more efficiently?

   Yes ☐ **No** ☐

 To do. I will ...

Use study time more efficiently

Check ✔ whether any of the factors below affect your study efficiency. Then consider where else you might waste time through the way you approach study. (Write them down so you remember them and take action!)

☐ Redoing tasks as I didn't first work out fully what was needed first

☐ Reading without absorbing it

☐ Stopping and starting tasks, interrupting my flow of thought

☐ Flitting between unrelated tasks

☐ Editing my writing because I didn't plan it well

☐ Editing my writing because I wrote more than I needed

☐ Taking too many breaks

☐ Taking too many notes

☐ Having to look things up again because of poor notes

☐ Not being systematic in the way I recorded references

☐ Having to follow up things I missed during lost class time

☐ Hunting for things I have lost (files, keys, book references, etc.)

☐ Revising for exams by simply reading through my notes

☐ Studying when I am too tired

Other things? List them!

47

Project plan for larger study tasks

Plan! Plan! Plan!

How does this help?

Most courses include a large assignment of some kind, such as a dissertation, long essay, portfolio or creative project. These enable you to gain an in-depth understanding of one aspect of the course, usually with personal choice. The large scale gives you opportunities to develop and showcase useful skills and qualities such as creativity, decision-making and meeting tight deadlines. It is meant to be challenging. It helps to use a project planning approach. Key factors in managing time on larger projects include making sound decisions about your focus, excellent planning, and taking a systematic, step-by-step approach.[32]

Considering your responses

If you feel anxious, vague or confused about what you need to do for a large project, be reassured that that is part of the process and you won't be alone. Start with a good plan, and much of the rest will fall into place.

 See also Ways 17, 20, 33, 49

 Do I ...?

1. Do I feel anxious about larger projects/ assignments?

   Yes ☐ **No** ☐

2. Do I have a topic already in mind?

   Yes ☐ **No** ☐

3. Do I understand the different time demands of undertaking a large project?

   Yes ☐ **No** ☐

 Find out more

Dissertations and Project Reports, Cottrell (2014)[32]

 To do. I will ...

Plot it step by step

Take it in your stride

Don't be overwhelmed by the size of the task. Break it into logical steps (see Way 20).

Scale it right

Many projects fail because they are too ambitious for the time, word-allowances or resources. Aim at a beautifully crafted project, with a clear focus. Cover a relatively small area in depth.

Allot time for every task

Know exactly how long you have for each step in the process. Working this out helps you check that you have chosen a project of the right scale.

Schedule in fine detail

Draw up a schedule that covers the entire length of the project. Allocate tasks to each day in a logical order, according to the time you allotted. Stick as closely as possible to your schedule – don't fall behind.

Take pride in your project

Invest yourself in the project you choose: enjoy it, take pride in the way you complete each step and what you learn, including from any mistakes. It helps you keep going.

Build in contingency time

Leave at least 10% unplanned time – to manage the unexpected.

48

Make smart use of time in exams

Allocate time in chunks and where it will count

Do I ...?

1. Do I complete the required number of questions in exams?

   Yes ☐ No ☐

2. Do I tend to write too much for some answers and not enough for others?

   Yes ☐ No ☐

3. Do I check my answers well?

   Yes ☐ No ☐

How does this help?

Exam success is not all about time management, but it helps. Just as good planning can help with exam preparation (Way 42), it is also important during the exam itself. Although most exam time is spent answering questions, there are other important tasks to undertake that can affect your grade. You need to spend time reading the questions carefully, grasping exactly what is required, deciding which questions to answer and in which order, deciding how much time to spend on each, checking your answers – and planning and monitoring your time wisely.[31]

 Find out more

The Exam Skills Handbook, Cottrell (2012)[31]

Considering your responses

If you don't usually allocate time well in exams, devise a good exam time strategy in advance and practise it beforehand. Work out timings for each question. Allocate time for tasks such as planning out answers, writing introductions and conclusions, and checking through your answers.

 To do. I will ...

 See also Ways 18, 23, 42

In exams – watch the clock!

Make a time plan

Plan in advance. In the exam room, jot down times to start and complete each question or section.

Time according to weighting

If all questions carry the same number of points, distribute time equally between them. If some are weighted more heavily (i.e. carry more marks or points), allocate time proportionally to reflect that.

Use your best sequence

... depending on whether you prefer to start with your best or worst answer, or to warm up with your second best.

Focus on the point

Take a moment to consider how tutors are likely to allocate points for each answer: what are they looking for? Don't just write everything you know on the topic. Make a quick plan to shape a well-constructed answer.

Plan time to check answers

... at the end. Don't spend all your time just answering the questions.

Attempt all required answers

Don't spend too much time on your favourite topic: recognise the point of diminishing returns in terms of marks awarded compared to time spent. You do better by attempting all the required questions.

Use all the available time

Read, check, reflect on and fine-tune answers. Recheck the exam paper to make sure you haven't misread any of it.

49 Prepare for life after study

Use time as a student to build a strong personal profile

How does this help?

The end of a course, which once seemed so far away, can arrive suddenly. It can come as a shock to find that other students have jobs or personal projects lined up already – if you haven't. It is harder to gain a job, especially a good one, if you wait until your final year; most of the best ones will be long gone. Your whole course and time as a student can contribute to preparing for time after graduation, whether that is a starter job, graduate scheme, a new career, promotion at work, further study or a personal project. Use resources provided through your uni or college to build your CV/résumé, ideally from the start of the course.

Considering your responses

If you are not preparing actively for your future, then it is wise to start a plan as soon as possible. Don't put off seeing a careers adviser if you don't (or do) know what you want to do: benefit from their advice.

 See also Ways 2, 6, 14, 17

 Do I ...?

1. Do I keep delaying seeing a careers adviser?

   Yes ☐ **No** ☐

2. Do I use time well for building a CV/résumé?

   Yes ☐ **No** ☐

3. Do I plan and prepare ahead to develop skills and qualities I will need for my future?

   Yes ☐ **No** ☐

 Find out more

Skills for Success, Cottrell (2015)[41]

 To do. I will ...

Make time to create opportunities

Start career planning early

You can't start too early – whether or not you know what career you want. Talk to a career adviser and get the ball rolling.

Have a job whilst studying

Employers like to see that you have experience of work, not least because it suggests you are used to the challenges of work environments.

More qualifications needed?

Check whether the kind of work that interests you requires further study. What do you need to do now to make sure you will be accepted onto courses at the next level?

Build your CV

Use your whole course to make and take opportunities that broaden your experience, skills and knowledge base. Decide which attributes will help you, and make opportunities to gain these.

Apply for jobs in good time

Don't wait until your final year: start applying in your penultimate year.

Explore your horizons

Plan time to research the different kinds of opportunities open to you after study. Taking a year out for interim jobs, travel, creative projects – or volunteering can be useful if you missed out on a good job during your final year.

50 Use time-saving tips and strategies

Share time-saving tips with others

? Do I …?

1. Do I look out for time-saving tips?

   Yes ☐ No ☐

2. Do I share time-saving tips with others?

   Yes ☐ No ☐

3. Do I know where in my week I could adopt time-saving strategies?

   Yes ☐ No ☐

How does this help?

Whilst there are some aspects of study where it is not advisable to use short-cuts, there are many ways of saving minutes here and there during the day. Over time, these can add up to hours or days! It can be fun to find and share time-saving strategies. Most simply involve some good organisation, use of the right resources and a little thought. What suits one person won't necessarily suit another: it takes trial and error to find strategies that suit you. Beware of ideas that cost you more time later. A few common time-savers are listed below to get you started. Share your own tips with other students and keep a list of your top 20 time-saving strategies on pages 112–13.

 Find out more

The Study Skills Handbook, Cottrell (2019)[17]

 To do. I will …

Considering your responses

If you don't already look out for time-saving strategies, then you might find that you can create more time than you expected, or at least use your time more efficiently. Sharing tips can be a good way of getting to know and help people, too!

 See also Ways 1, 9, 23, 32

Try out time-savers that others find useful

Decide ✔ which time-saving strategies you want to use.

Organisation for study

Use a 'see-at-a-glance' approach

- Week-to-view diary
- See-at-a-glance timetable
- See-at-a-glance syllabus
- See-through page protectors
- Folders labelled on spine
- Colour-coding material
- Well-organised folders
- Using folder dividers

All in one place
Enable fast-checking by collating key course information into an easy-to-carry diary/planner.

Find the 'sweet spot'
Don't overdo time-saving strategies – too much time spent organising, making timetables and writing lists can turn them into time-wasters.

Share study tasks
Lighten the load![17] See Way 37 and *The Study Skills Handbook*, Cottrell (2019).

When making notes

Use descriptive headers
Use section, page and paragraph headers in your notes. Make clear what the material is about, so you can browse and find it at speed.

Check before noting
Have you made similar notes on this topic already from a different source? If so, could you just cross-reference to your other notes?

Don't just 'tidy' notes

Avoid rewriting or typing them just to make them look neater. Typically, students start to do this on autopilot without learning much. Instead, use more active note-making strategies that engage you in deeper thought.[17]

Keep detailed records of sources

Every time you use a source that looks useful, note all the details you would need for your references if you cite it in an assignment.

Digital life

Select time-saving apps

Keep an eye out for reviews of student apps, or see annual updates in *The Macmillan Student Planner*. There are apps to cover many aspects of study, from note-making to storing references (see pages 115–16).

Limit internet time

If you can't do it through willpower alone, then use free apps such as SelfControl to block your use of whatever websites and media take up too much of your time.

Avoid online distraction in class

Otherwise, it just means having to spend time later working out what you missed and catching up – and that takes longer than if you focus the first time round.

Adopt the right mindset

Avoid 'worry time'

It doesn't get anything done. Divert the energy into activity instead – whether study or fun. You'll be less stressed and more productive.[40]

Don't spend time in regrets

If you mess up on time management (or other aspects of your study) put it down to experience rather than feeling bad about it. Learn from your mistakes. Start afresh from now.

Complete half-finished tasks
... so you don't have to keep thinking about them. If they don't need to be done, cross them off your list.

Organisation for life

Organise your bag/backpack
Keep things in the same place in your bag for speedy retrieval. Keep your bag or backpack stocked with pens and essential daily items for a quick exit in the morning.

Use a standard shopping list
Do it once and copy. Add items by exception.

Make a weekly meal planner
Cook enough for several meals. Exchange meals with friends.

Stock up on essentials
... such as basic foodstuffs and toiletries. Save time making multiple trips to stock up.

Do one thing at a time
You make fewer mistakes.

Plan your daily route
... so you cover errands on the fastest route as you go.

Use a timer
Set alerts so that you don't let phone calls, games, etc. over-run.

Use washi tape to sort items
... and to spot them at speed – such as for electrical items and their chargers. Keep long cords wound up and bound so they don't tangle. Label chargers and plugs in case they become separated.

Habits shaper: Track your good intentions

Draw together your entries from the 'I will' boxes. Jot down the page number for easy cross reference. Select those you are keenest to do. Add a star, emoticon or **highlighting** each time you act on your intention.

I have committed to doing...	Way	Page
☺		
☺		
☺		
☺		

I have committed to doing...		Way	Page
	☺		
	☺		
	☺		
	☺		
	☺		

My progress so far

Keep track of which of these 50 Ways you have started and completed (✔). If you come back to the book after a break, you can see at a glance which aspects you had intended to pursue, and decide whether to take up from where you left off.

Way	Page	Short title	Doing	Done!
1	2	Take your time power		
2	4	'What's in it for me?'		
3	6	Identify your time-management priorities		
4	10	Know your time demons		
5	12	Make friends with time		
6	14	Spend time where you will value it the most		
7	16	Make well-timed decisions		
8	18	Tune in to your time wisdom		
9	20	Use the right 'time tools'		
10	22	Learn the flow of the academic year		
11	24	Take time to adapt to the course		
12	26	Create a realistic study timetable		
13	28	Manage your procrastination!		
14	30	Be guided by your goals		
15	32	Style your day		
16	34	Plan enough downtime		
17	36	Use smart pacing and forward planning		
18	38	Speed-task it!		
19	40	Build study stamina		
20	42	Break it down!		
21	44	Cue yourself in!		
22	48	Visualise it		
23	50	Don't spare your spare minutes!		

List of 20+ favourite time-saving tips ...

List at least 20 ways that good time management could benefit your study,
well-being and career.

1

2

3

4

5

6

7

8

9

10

11

12

13

14

15

16

17

18

19

20

Where to find out more

Citing/referencing sources

www.citethisforme.com/harvard-referencing (free reference tool for Harvard style references).

www.mendeley.com/reference-management/reference-manager (free referencing tool).

www.zotero.org/ (free referencing tool).

Diary management

Cottrell, S. (updated annually). *The Macmillan Student Planner* (London: Red Globe Press). (For organising all aspects of life as a student.)

Exams

Cottrell, S. (2012). *The Exam Skills Handbook: Achieving Peak Performance* (2nd edn) (London: Red Globe Press).

Mindfulness

Cottrell, S. (2018). *Mindfulness for Students* (London: Red Globe Press).

Online meditations at: www. macmillanihe.com/mindfulness

Twitter
#mindful

#mindfulness
#mindfulstudent

Organising your space

Aparto admin (2018). *10 Space-Saving Tips to Help Organise Your Room.*

https://apartostudent.com/blog/10-space-saving-tips-help-organise-room

Planning out assignments

Cottrell, S. (2019). *The Study Skills Handbook* (5th edn) (London: Red Globe Press). Guidance, tips and templates for a step-by-step approach to writing essays and other assignments.

Cottrell, S. (2014). *Dissertations and Project Reports: A Step by Step Guide.* (London: Red Globe Press).

Planning for your future

Cottrell, S. (2015). *Skills for Success: Personal Development and Employability* (3rd edn) (London: Red Globe Press).

https://nationalcareersservice.direct.gov.uk/

www.prospects.ac.uk/careers-advice

Relaxing time

www.mind.org.uk/information-support/
tips-for-everyday-living/relaxation/#.
W9qvxXv7Spo

https://videos.pexels.com/search/
nature (wide range of free short nature
videos).

https://pixabay.com/en/videos/
list/?cat=nature (free short nature videos).

https://lusity.en.uptodown.com/
android (relaxing sounds for calm, rest
and sleep).

www.verywellfit.com/relaxing-total-
body-stretches-1231150 (eight relaxing
body stretches, with videos).

www.brokeandhealthy.com/ (100 free
or cheap ways to exercise).

Study skills

Cottrell, S. (2019). *The Study Skills Handbook* (5th edn) (London: Red Globe Press).

Cottrell, S. (2019). *50 Ways to Boost Your Grades* (London: Red Globe Press).

Cottrell, S. (2017). *Critical Thinking Skills* (3rd edn) (London: Red Globe Press).

Cottrell, S. (2019). *50 Ways to Excel at Writing* (London: Red Globe Press).

Macmillan free study skills site: www. thestudyspace.com

Twitter

@cottrell_study

#SuccessfulStudent

#StudyTip

#amwriting

#mindfulstudent

Talks and articles about time

Podcast

iProcrastinate hosts a Podcast hosted by Pychyl

6 Incredible TED Talks About Time Management (Brightpod).

www.brightpod.com/boost/6-
incredible-ted-talks-about-time-
management

Tim Urban (Feb 2016) www.ted.com/
talks/tim_urban_inside_the_mind_of_a_
master_procrastinator?

Blogs/articles

Locke, S. Why your brain loves procrastination. Updated by Susannah Locke @susannahlocke Apr 18, 2016, 2:00pm EDT. www.vox.com/
2014/12/8/7352833/
procrastination-psychology-help-stop

Time management tools

Apps

www.topuniversities.com/blog/best-
time-management-apps-students

Diary/Planner

Cottrell, S. (updated annually). *The Macmillan Student Planner* (London: Red Globe Press). (Contains week-to-view diary pages, year-to-view planner, study organisers, life organisers, and other material relevant to student life.)

Project planning

Spilker, J. (2017). 18 Best Gantt Chart Software to Transform Your Project Management in 2018 (18 August) www.workzone.com/blog/gantt-chart-software/

Well-being

Health and mental health

https://apps.beta.nhs.uk/ (a wide range of free apps from the NHS on many aspects of health).

www.happify.com/

www.mentalhealth.org.uk

www.mind.org.uk

Help and support

NHS www.nhs.uk/Service-Search/Psychological-therapies-(IAPT)/LocationSearch/10008

www.studentminds.org.uk/findsupport.html

Nightline www.nightline.ac.uk/

Self-massage

www.csp.org.uk/public-patient/rehabilitation-exercises/shoulder-pain

www.csp.org.uk/publications/neck-pain-exercises

Sleep

www.nhs.uk/live-well/sleep-and-tiredness/10-tips-to-beat-insomnia/

Stress

Cottrell, S. (2019). *50 Ways to Manage Stress* (London: Red Globe Press).

www.nhs.uk/choices (Student Stress: Self-help tips. Includes links to 8 free mental well-being podcasts and audio guides).

References and bibliography

References

1. Risko, V. J., Alvarez, M. C. and Fairbank, M. M. (1991). 'External factors that influence study'. In R. F. Flippo and D. C. Caverly (eds.), *Teaching, Reading and Study Strategies at College Level* (Navark, D. E.: International Reading Association), pp. 195–236.

2. Nist, S. L., Simpson, M. L., Olejnik, S. and Mealey, D. L. (1991). 'The relationship between self-selected processes and test performances'. *American Educational Research Journal*, 28(4), pp. 849–74.

3. Tanriogen, A. and Iscan, S. (2009). 'Time management skills of Pamukkale University students and their effects on academic achievement'. *Eurasian Journal of Educational Research* (EJER), 35, pp. 93–108.

4. Thibodeaux, J., Deutsch, A. and Kitsantas, A. (2016). 'First-year college students' time use. Relations with self-regulation and GPA'. *Journal of Advanced Academics*, 28(1), pp. 5–27.

5. Al Khatib, A. S. (2014). 'Time management and its relation to students' stress, gender and academic achievement among sample of students at Al Ain University of Science and Technology, UAE'. *International Journal of Business and Social Research* (IJBSR), 4(5), pp. 47–58.

6. Britton, B. K. and Tesser, A. (1991). 'Effects of time management practices on college grades'. *Journal of Educational Psychology*, 83, pp. 405–10.

7. Misra, R. and McKean, M. (2000). 'College students' academic stress and its relation to their anxiety, time management, and leisure satisfaction'. *American Journal of Health Studies*, 16(1), pp. 41–51.

8. Eldeleklioğlu, J. (2008). 'Investigation of adolescents' time-management skills in terms of anxiety, age and gender variables'. *Elementary Education Online*, 7(3), pp. 656–63.

9. Kaya, H., Kaya, N., Palloş, A. Ö. and Küçük, L. (2012). 'Assessing time-management skills in terms of age, gender, and anxiety levels: A study on nursing and midwifery students in Turkey'. *Nurse Educ Pract.* 12(5), pp. 284–8.

10. Wahat, N. H. A., Saat, N. Z. M., Ching, C. K., Qin, L. Y., May, G. C. and Omar, N. (2012). 'Time management skill and stress level among audiology and speech sciences students of Universiti Kebangsaan Malaysia'. *Procedia – Social and Behavioral Sciences*, 59, pp. 704–8. Electronic physician p. 3683.

11. Wright, K. P. Jr., Hull, J. T., Hughes, R. J., Ronda, J. M. and Czeisler, C. A. (2006). 'Sleep and wakefulness out of phase with internal biological time impairs learning in humans'. *J. Cog. Neurosci.* 18, pp. 508–21.

12. Nasri, S. H., Pazargadi, M., Zagheri Tafreshi, M. and Nassiri, N. (2013). 'The correlation of head nurses' time management with nurses' job satisfaction in medical & surgical wards of hospitals in Arak Medical Sciences University'. *Journal of Nursing and Midwifery*, 22(79), pp. 1–7.

13. Lay, C. H. and Schouwenburg, H. C. (1993). 'Trait procrastination, time management, and academic behaviour'. *Journal of Social Behavior and Personality*, January, 8(4).
14. Macan, T. H., Shahini, C., Dipboye, R. L. and Phillips, A. P. (1990). 'College students' time management: correlations with academic performance and stress'. *Journal of Educational Psychology*, 82, pp. 760–8.
15. Pehlivan, A. (2013). 'The effect of the time management skills of students taking a financial accounting course on their course grades and grade point averages. Irregular sleep/wake patterns are associated with poorer academic performance and delayed circadian and sleep/wake timing'. *Scientific Reports*, 7, no. 3216 (2017).
16. Cottrell, S. (2018). *Mindfulness for Students* (London: Red Globe Press).
17. Cottrell, S. (2019). *The Study Skills Handbook* (5th edn) (London: Red Globe Press).
18. Leone, M. L., Slezak, D. M., Golombek, D. and Sigman, M. (2016). 'Time to decide: Diurnal variations on the speed and quality of human decisions'. *Cognition*, 158, pp. 44–55.
19. Kouchaki, M. and Smith, I. H. (2013). 'The morning morality effect: The influence of time of day on unethical behavior'. *Psychological Science*, 25(1), pp. 95–102.
20. Danziger, S., Levav, J. and Avnaim-Pesso, L. (2011). 'Extraneous factors in judicial decisions'. *Proceedings of the National Academy of Sciences of the USA*, 108(17), pp. 6889–92.
21. Cottrell, S. (updated annually). *The Macmillan Student Planner* (London: Red Globe Press).
22. Tice, D. M. and Ferrari, J. R. (2000). 'Procrastination as a self-handicap for men and women: A task-avoidance strategy in a laboratory setting'. *Journal of Research in Personality*, 34(1), pp. 73–83.
23. Tice, D. M., Bratslavsky, E. and Baumeister, R. F. (2001). 'Motional distress regulation takes precedence over impulse control: If you feel bad, do it!' *Journal of Personal and Social Psychology*, 80(1), pp. 53–67.
24. Pychyl, T. A. and Flett, G. L. (2012). 'Procrastination and self-regulatory failure: An introduction to the special issue'. *Journal of Rational Emotive and Cognitive Behavior Therapy*, 30, pp. 203–12.
25. Tice, D. M. and Baumeister, R. F. (1997). 'Longitudinal study of procrastination, performance, stress, and health: The costs and benefits of dawdling'. *Psychological Science*, 8, pp. 454–8.
26. Wohl, M. J. A., Pychyl, T. A. and Bennett, S. H. (2010). 'I forgive myself, now I can study: How self-forgiveness for procrastinating can reduce future procrastination'. *Personality and Individual Differences*, 48, pp. 803–8.
27. Hershfield, H. E. (2011). 'Future self-continuity: How conceptions of the future self transform intertemporal choice'. *Annals of the New York Academy of Sciences*, October 2011, 1235(1).
28. Phillips, A. J. K., Clery, W. M., O'Brien, C. S., Sano, A., Berger, L. K., Picard, R. W., Lockley, S. W., Klerman, E. B. and Czeisler, C. A. (2017). 'Irregular sleep/wake patterns are associated with poorer academic performance and delayed circadian and sleep/wake timing'. *Scientific Reports*, 7, no. 3216.
29. Medeiros, A. L. D., Mendes, D. B. F., Lima, P. F. and Araujo, J. F. (2010). 'The relationships between sleep-wake cycle and academic performance in medical students'. *Biol. Rhythm Res*, 32, pp. 263–70.

30. Immordino-Yang, M. H., Christodoulou, J. A. and Singh, V. (2012). 'Rest is not idleness: Implications of the brain's default mode for human development and education'. *Perspectives on Psychological Science, 7*(4), pp. 352–64.
31. Cottrell, S. (2012). *The Exam Skills Handbook* (2nd edn) (London: Red Globe Press).
32. Cottrell, S. (2014). *Dissertations and Project Reports: A Step by Step Guide* (London: Red Globe Press).
33. Mark, G., Gudith, J. and Klocke, U. (2008). 'The cost of interrupted work: More speed and stress'. *Proceedings of the SIGCHI Conference on Human Factors in Computing Systems*, pp. 107–10.
34. Ophir, E., Nass, C. and Wagner, A. D. (2009). 'Cognitive control in media-multitaskers'. In *Proceedings of the National Academy of Sciences of the United States of America*, 106(35), pp. 15583–7.
35. Pixie Technology Inc. (2017). *Lost and Found: The Average American Spends 2.5 Days Each Year Looking For Lost Items* [online]. 2 May, Available at: https://getpixie.com/pages/lost-and-found [Accessed 19 January 2019].
36. Vohs, K. D., Redden, J. P. and Rahinel, R. (2013). 'Physical order produces healthy choices, generosity, and conventionality, whereas disorder produces creativity'. *Psychological Science,* 24(9), pp. 1860–7.
37. Hosie, R. (2017). 'The key to finding anything you've lost, according to a new study'. *The Independent* [online], 22 February 2017, Available at: www.independent.co.uk/life-style/lost-found-property-keys-how-to-find-study-university-aberdeen-clutter-a7593331.html [Accessed 19 January 2019].
38. Wieber, F., Thürmer, J. L. and Gollwitzer, P. M. (2015). 'Promoting the translation of intentions into action by implementation intentions: Behavioral effects and physiological correlates'. *Frontiers in Human Neuroscience,* 9, p. 395.
39. Kreijns, K., Kalz, M., Castano-Munoz, J. and Punie, Y. (2017). 'Implementation intention and how it affects goal achievement in MOOCs'. [online] Available at: https://dspace.ou.nl/bitstream/1820/7889/1/IIGoals-eMOOCs17-final.pdf [Accessed 19 January 2019].
40. Cottrell, S. (2019). *50 Ways to Manage Stress* (London: Red Globe Press).
41. Cottrell, S. (2015). *Skills for Success* (3rd edn) (London: Red Globe Press).

Bibliography

Cottrell, S. (2017). *Critical Thinking Skills* (3rd edn) (London: Red Globe Press).

Jahanseir, K., Salehzadeh, K., Vesagi, H. and Mosavifar, A. (2008). 'A study of the effect of time management on academic achievement of students of Islamic Azad University Maragheh Branch'. *Research in Curriculum Planning,* 1(16), pp. 97–114.

Kelly, W. E. (2003). 'No time to worry: The relationship between worry, time structure, and time management'. *Personality and Individual Differences,* 35(5), pp. 1119–26.

Index

Notes

Notes